Recovering from Psychosis

The use of first-hand service user accounts of mental illness is still limited in the professional literature available. This is, however, beginning to change, with a new 'recovery' focus in mental health services meaning that the voices of service users are finally being heard. *Recovering from Psychosis: Empirical Evidence and Lived Experience* synthesises a narrative approach alongside an evidence-based review of current treatment by including Stephen Williams' own personal experience as it relates to psychosis, recovery and treatment. A mental health professional himself, the author's account of his own recovery from severe mental health difficulties, without sustained intervention, challenges the orthodoxy of representation of service users in mental health.

Recovering from Psychosis critically explores and reviews the current state of the art of research and knowledge about the nature and treatment of psychosis. Working simultaneously from empirical, lived experience and philosophical perspectives, Stephen Williams:

- Evaluates political and power-related issues in professional understanding, knowledge-creation and treatment of people with psychosis;
- Introduces the current 'recovery movement', unpacking its origins and implications for the future development of 'recovery oriented services';
- Reviews, summarizes and critiques the current state of 'recovery' research, looking at the advantages and disadvantages of such an approach, examining how this is influencing the transformation of UK mental health services;
- Analyses the difficulties in organisational implementation of recovery approaches, summarises the most empirically robust approaches to practice, personal and service delivery measurement;
- Reviews current 'models' of psychosis and how various professional scientific groups explain the experience and nature of psychosis;
- Uses lived-experience accounts taken from the scientific literature, portraying the nature of such experiences and analysing them in the face of contemporary psychological models.

Recovering from Psychosis is an essential comprehensive guide for mental health professionals, psychologists, social workers and carers, who are working with people with severe and enduring mental health difficulties diagnosed as psychosis. It addresses the practical implications of working with such difficult conditions and serves as a hopeful story of recovery for service users.

Stephen Williams is a Lectu   y of Bradford.

"A very powerful tome. Much of the literature is familiar and his analysis of the current ideas are comprehensive and thought provoking. I found it a relaxed and easy read, despite its topic. By that I didn't have to work too hard to understand what was being said. It was coherent and followed a helpful trajectory. I was engrossed in chapter three and it was helpful how his narrative was punctuated with academic analysis. What a sad, yet powerful transformative story."

– Nigel Short, Informal Associate, School of Psychology, University of Sussex, UK and co-editor of *Contemporary British Autoethnography*

Recovering from Psychosis

Empirical Evidence and Lived Experience

Stephen Williams

Routledge
Taylor & Francis Group

LONDON AND NEW YORK

First published 2016
by Routledge
2 Park Square, Milton Park, Abingdon, Oxon, OX14 4RN

And by Routledge
711 Third Avenue, New York, NY 10017

Routledge is an imprint of the Taylor & Francis Group, an informa business

British Library Cataloguing in Publication Data
A catalogue record for this book is available from the British Library

Library of Congress Cataloging-in-Publication Data
CIP data has been applied for

ISBN: 978-0-415-82204-6 (hbk)
ISBN: 978-0-415-82205-3 (pbk)
ISBN: 978-0-203-56759-3 (ebk)

Typeset in Times
by Apex CoVantage, LLC

Printed and bound by Ashford Colour Press Ltd., Gosport, Hampshire.

MIX
Paper from
responsible sources
FSC® C011748

When no idea seems right, the right one must seem wrong.
Marvin Minsky (1981), 'Music, Mind, and Meaning'

I'd like to dedicate this book to my wife, Dawn Williams, who has been unswervingly and unstintingly supportive of my near workaholic tendencies.

Cover illustration

The cover illustration is the work of Nick Gebbett, who kindly granted me permission to use his painting depicting aspects of the experience of psychosis. Nick is a contemporary artist/painter based in Brighton whose work can be found at http://nicholasgebbettarts.jimdo.com/.

Contents

Acknowledgements

This book could not have been written without the kind encouragement and support of my colleagues and students at the University of Bradford. I would particularly like to thank David Streatfield for helpful and stimulating conversations about my own experience of emotional distress and recovery. I'd like to thank my colleague Steve Bates for his carefully considered critique of the manuscript. Laura-Middleton Green, Melissa Owens and Ian Hodgson are the core of our Shut Up and Write group that proved instrumental in helping me cultivate some kind of discipline in my writing. I'd like to thank Joanne Forshaw and Kirsten Buchanan for their helpful editorial guidance and the patience of the Routledge team throughout the production of this book.

The quotation from Marvin Minsky's (1981) 'Music, Mind, and Meaning' is reproduced with the kind permission of Springer Science + Business Media New York, Music, Mind, and Brain: The Neuropsychology of Music, Manfred Clynes, ed. (© 1982 Springer Science + Business Media New York, DOI: 10.1007/978-1-4684-8917-0 ISBN: 978-1-4684-8919-4).

Foreword

A new cultural space is opening up in mental health research, scholarship and writing internationally. Within this space, hybrid, transcultural standpoint identity is enabling different and fresh ways of engaging with the knowledge and practice domain of recovery. Originating in postcolonial studies, the concept of cultural hybridity points to new forms of 'hyphenated' identity in mental health writing, in the emergence of work undertaken by scholar-user-survivor-teacher-practitioners (Grant and Leigh-Phippard, 2014). Hybrid scholarship challenges the hegemony of exclusively professional, empirical and policy-led knowledge, while positively undermining traditional barriers between mental health professionals and those in receipt of their care.

Hybrid scholarship in mental health is currently represented in several interrelated paradigmatic, theoretical and methodological developments. The lived experience paradigm provides both an alternative and complementary body of knowledge to so-called gold-standard positivist, outcome-based work. The reflexivity inherent in lived-experience work paves the way for the utilization and development of progressive qualitative methodologies such as autoethnography (Grant, Short and Turner, 2013). Such relatively new forms of narrative inquiry, in turn, provide mental health users and survivors possibilities for re-storying their future identities in hopeful, compassionate and existentially fulfilling ways (Grant and Leigh-Phippard, 2014).

However, in developing cultures engaged in postcolonial struggles, the emergence of politically and intellectually active hybrid citizens – the product of relationships between the colonizers and indigenous peoples – often proves a threat to the established power structures and hierarchies imposed by the original colonizers. This tends to result in colonizers' increasing their efforts to maintain their traditional power base and a continued clear separation between 'them' and 'us'. Such a trend parallels the kinds of reactions that are already evident in many mental health circles internationally, where lived-experience knowledge is often disparaged, for example, as 'anecdata'. The implicit message conveyed in such reactions is that service users and self-proclaimed 'survivors' should know their place.

This implicit message is also currently enshrined in UK mental health nursing policy, which frames 'recovery' on the basis of the tacitly accepted authority of institutional psychiatry. The 'Chief Nursing Officer's Review of Mental Health Nursing' (DOH 2006) "constructs the gender neutral, compliant, homogenized and relatively silent recovering patient in keeping with . . . its own circular logic: that specialist nursing staff in specialist work settings know best what recovery means in the context of their professional and environmental specialisms" (Grant and Leigh-Phippard, 2014, pp. 103–4).

In the face of the emergence of new, transcultural ways of making sense of the meaning and process of recovery, continued reactionary tendencies from professional and policy-making groups in mental health are understandable. But this new paradigm is gathering strength to an extent that future mental health workers, research and policy developers and consumer constituencies will find increasingly difficult to ignore or disparage.

This new text by Stephen Williams is an exemplar in this regard, celebrating paradigmatic change around recovery inquiry in rigorous hybrid scholarship. Eminently readable, it manages to balance the empirical, theoretical and discursive with an autoethnographic strand woven throughout the book in a finessed and sophisticated way. Williams evaluates current and key empirical, theoretical and philosophical work in mental health recovery from both the context of his own psychotic breakdown as a young man, his subsequent involvement in institutional psychiatric care and personal recovery journey, and his current position as a mental health nursing scholar and teacher in UK Higher Education.

The resulting text contains several interwoven narratives within which Williams' own transcultural and intellectual integrity is never compromised. This accords him the authority to review UK and international approaches to understanding, working with and recovering from psychosis from post- and trans-modern positions, to address the often neglected political dimensions of recovery, and, with an eye to the future, to look at a future landscape 'beyond recovery'.

This courageous and novel text will, I predict, prove to be of enduring and vital importance for mental health nurses and other mental health professionals and recovery researchers, as well as for survivor, user and carer groups across many countries.

Alec Grant, PhD
Reader in Narrative Mental Health
School of Health Sciences
University of Brighton, UK

Chapter 1

The aims and intentions of recovering from psychosis

Empirical evidence and lived experience

The overarching aim of this book is to critically review the state of empirical evidence that explores the nature of recovery in relation to psychosis. A reflective semi-autobiographical commentary on the empirical evidence forms a critical 'lived experience' perspective. This book is primarily intended for mental health nurses but should also be of interest to other mental health professionals, regardless of their specific professional orientation, who have an interest in the development of mental health care in the light of the emerging 'recovery' approach. This chapter also provides a chapter-by-chapter guide of the topics addressed and the kinds of critique used and sources of information explored.

Chapter 2, 'Introduction to Psychosis, Recovery, Post-Modernity and Trans-Modernity', provides an introduction to the principal topic areas of psychosis and recovery. It explores the particular challenges of defining psychosis in the context of the philosophy of science. It also provides a lived experience account that is developed in subsequent chapters. This 'autoethnographic' approach serves to add colour through the author's personal testimony of his lived experience. The lived experience sections, provided in shaded text boxes, act, in a sense, as case examples of the particular aspects of psychosis and recovery being explored as the book unfolds. At times, they are examined by the author in the context of the various explanatory models that are used in psychiatry and psychology in particular. Examples are also provided from the author's clinical experience with the application of interventions and models that are under empirical scrutiny. For example, a first-hand account of using cognitive-behavioural therapy for unusual beliefs is explored in Chapter 4.

The chapter goes on to explore the rise and meaning of 'recovery' as applied to mental health services, and this is similarly explored from a lived experience perspective. Recovery is critically reflected upon; the potential benefits are raised but also the risks, particularly as they pertain to the development of mental health nursing. The chapter concludes by introducing the philosophical critical stances of post-modernism and trans-modernism as they apply to mental health practice.

Chapter 3, 'An Autoethnographic Account of Psychosis in the Context of Neurobiological, Cognitive Psychological and Meta-Synthetic Analysis', is in many regards a pivotal gateway chapter that informs the entire book. It begins with my lived experience account of developing psychosis and attempts to synthesize into this pertinent aspects of the empirical evidence. The increasingly recognized role of trauma is reviewed that has placed new emphasis on the psychosocial aspects of psychosis within what has previously been a more biologically emphasized aetiology. Relevant aspects of neurobiological, psychological, neurocognitive, neuro-computational theory and research into the genetics of psychosis are reviewed and explored, and where possible this is related to the lived experience perspective. The chapter overall intends to present both the personal perspective and an overview of current scientific models of psychosis across a range of disciplines that inform mental health care.

Chapter 4, 'A Review of Current UK Treatment Approaches to Psychosis: Surveying Contemporary Interventions and Their Empirical Status', seeks to provide a review of the empirical status of the mainstay of treatment interventions for psychosis. It explores the different kinds of psychological interventions being developed and used. Interventions developed from the neurocognitive theories of psychosis are evaluated, as are the rise of third-wave 'contextual' cognitive psychological interventions (Grant et al., 2010; Hayes, 2004) – e.g. Acceptance and Commitment and Mindfulness. A first-hand clinical experience account of delivering cognitive-behavioural therapy for psychosis is given, along with a review of the empirical evidence. The chapter concludes with a review of the empirical evidence underpinning the use of antipsychotic medication, and this is presented alongside a lived experience account of the use of medication.

Chapter 5, 'Research into Recovery from Psychosis: An Empirical Review and Critical Reflection', provides an overview of the current state of recovery research. It critically reflects on the rise of recovery research and the disjunction that also exists in its application to practice. Key pieces of research are discussed in detail: the development of the CHIME conceptual framework (Leamy et al., 2011), coping strategies derived from qualitative research (Phillips et al., 2009) and a review of guidance for recovery-oriented practice (Le Boutillier et al., 2011). The components of recovery-oriented practice are also reviewed in the light of emerging research (Slade et al., 2011), including supporting goal striving (Clarke et al., 2009), evidence-based coaching (Grant and Cavanagh, 2007) and the principles of a collaborative recovery model (Oades et al., 2009). The state of evidence for the rise of recovery colleges is also reviewed, and the challenges to mental health practices and research are explored in the context of this new 'paradigm'.

Chapter 6, 'Recovery, Psychosis and Identity', explores the important role that identity has in the experience of psychosis and subsequent recovery. Current psychosocial understanding of the nature of identity is explored in detail, and this is linked to previous qualitative evidence on the nature of psychosis (McCarthy-Jones et al., 2013). The interplay between experiences of psychosis and psychological models is explored in relation to the impact the condition can have on a person's identity and security of self in particular. This leads to some discussion of how current psychological interventions can attend and support the reforging of the self. An overview of narrative theory as a strand of psychological approach is reviewed and placed in the context of identity and psychosis. The wider implications of social role and stigma are addressed and this is illustrated with my lived experience account of recovery. The chapter ends with a discussion of how the organizational context of mental health services creates certain barriers to recovery.

Chapter 7, 'Political Dimensions of Recovery', builds on organizational issues to reflect critically in increased depth on some of the obstacles that mental health services face in adopting a transformative recovery-oriented approach. It addresses the difficulties of implementing recovery and the particular challenges of legal frameworks such as the Community Treatment Order (Burns and Molodynski, 2014). It also addresses certain professional misapprehensions about recovery and what organizations must tackle to develop a partnership approach to service delivery. Current political issues are used to highlight the real dangers for the potential abuse of the recovery approach.

Chapter 8, 'Measuring Recovery: The Tyranny of Psychometry', addresses the inevitable need of statutory services to measure and produce evidence of the impact of recovery-oriented practices. A post-modernist critical appraisal is made of the assumptions inherent in the application of measurements practices. A brief empirical review and critique are then given of the state of research measures of service recovery orientation and measures of personal recovery. The chapter goes on to explore what recovery measures might be capturing and how this does or does not fit with espoused recovery values – i.e. of narrative recovery and 're-authoring'.

Chapter 9, 'Beyond Recovery: Towards Mental Health as Well-Being', seeks to signpost where the development of recovery-oriented services seems to be heading. It charts the rise and promise of positive psychology and places these ideas into the wider context of health and illness. A brief review of the empirical status of positive psychological interventions is then given, and a specific example of interventions that seek to integrate a well-being- and resilience-focused approach into practice is outlined. Some of the emerging resistance and difficulties with a well-being-oriented approach are discussed, and the role of digital communities is addressed as a new frontier of mental health practice.

Chapter 10, 'Reflections upon Recovery: The Person Is Political', seeks to synthesize the main themes and issues covered in the preceding nine chapters. It highlights the risks inherent in the translation by research and academia of recovery into the realities of service users' lives and clinical practice. It emphasizes the need for valuing storytelling on a variety of levels and reflects on the pitfalls and limitations of current treatment approaches. It takes stock of the state of recovery research and what it has to say about the role of identity, growth and well-being as fundamental topics of concern for mental health clinical practice.

The overarching aim of this volume is to provide a robust empirical review of the state of evidence surrounding the principal topics of recovery and psychosis. It also seeks to raise the profile of qualitative and lived experience accounts of these subjects. In addition, it seeks to critically reflect upon the status of empirical research and the inherent assumptions that are made in their undertaking. You will find that the portions of the book containing lived experience accounts (in shaded text boxes) are presented in the context of the critical review of the empirical research that they speak to.

Chapter 2

Introduction to psychosis, recovery, post-modernity and trans-modernity

This chapter introduces the principal topic areas of psychosis, recovery and post-modernity. It provides definitions of these terms and explores some of the relevant contextual issues. Recovery and psychosis are introduced from a critical evidence-based standpoint, from a post-modernist and at times a trans-modern perspective and from a lived experience first-person perspective.

The challenge of defining psychosis

The World Health Organization (WHO) and Royal College of Psychiatrists (RCP) both recognize that psychosis is a component of so-called severe mental illness (SMI), although there is little consensus over what this specifically means (Ruggeri et al., 2000). The RCP identify that losing contact with reality is a defining feature of psychosis (RCP, 2012), whereas the WHO (1992) states that it "indicates the presence of hallucinations, delusions, or a limited number of severe abnormalities of behaviour, such as gross excitement and overactivity, marked psychomotor retardation, and catatonic behaviour" (p. 10).

Ruggeri et al. (2000) operationalize this definition of SMI: "a patient has severe mental illness when he or she has the following: a diagnosis of any non-organic psychosis; a duration of treatment of two years or more; dysfunction, as measured by the Global Assessment of Functioning (GAF) scale" (American Psychiatric Association, 1987; cited in Ruggeri et al., 2000, p. 149). In these definitions, experiences of psychosis that are associated with a specific organic cause (e.g. as in the dementias or acquired brain injury) are differentiated from so-called functional psychoses where no apparent structural or physical causal precipitant can be identified. In this narrow sense, a functional psychosis is construed as a necessary constituent of SMI. This doesn't get us much closer to understanding what psychosis is *like*, however, or what it is, and it presents a clearly circular argument. In this account, psychosis is a *kind* of SMI, and an SMI is, by this definition, one that includes a *sufficient degree and kind* of psychosis.

This tautology exposes a long-recognized fundamental flaw in the attempts to develop psychiatry as a scientific discipline. Science carves up the domains of study into *kinds* and theorizes about them (Quine, 1969). It has been keenly debated, particularly in the last 40 years of metaphysics and philosophy, as to whether special sciences such as psychology and psychiatry satisfy the conditions for 'natural-kindhood' (see Fodor, 1974; Dupre, 1993). Special sciences are all those that are presumed to be reducible to physics (Fodor, 1974). A fundamental question posed by the philosophy of science is whether the kinds classified by psychiatry are *scientifically real*. By this, they mean do they correspond to real kinds in nature?

The emergence of a substrain of medicine and psychiatry that proclaims itself to be 'values-based' is one of the reactions to the developing understanding that conceptualizing elements of the human condition as mental illness is not successfully "carving nature at its joints" (Slade, 2009, p. 18). A values-oriented approach directs us to consider diagnosis as a way of understanding and talking about things rather than as an explanation per se. Consider the difference in saying to a person, 'You have a psychosis', as opposed to, 'Your experiences can be understood as psychosis'. The former statement implies that psychosis is a *real thing to be had* and proclaims the diagnosis as scientifically (and thus ontologically) valid rather than a vehicle to promote communication/understanding. These are radically different stances on the causal validity of diagnosis.

So psychosis is perhaps more helpfully viewed as a construction of psychiatry. This is not to be mistaken for invalidating the reality of the emotional distress of such diagnoses. It is instead an acknowledgement that this is simply a means of taxonomizing and individuating people who meet certain categorical criteria at a certain point in time. It provides a means of identifying them as belonging to a certain group. A 'strong' post-modernist argument is that it serves to create and perpetuate that group. It does little, however, to represent the rich variety of people and their experiences (of psychosis) that make them different from others who are given that label and indeed from others who are not.

A LIVED EXPERIENCE PERSPECTIVE OF WHAT PSYCHOSIS MEANS

My own experience of psychosis was that the nature of my thinking was such that at times it *changed* my experience of reality. So I present an alternative hypothesis, by virtue of lived experience: psychosis is where the process of interpreting events (both internal and external) is so catastrophically disrupted that the lens of personally held meaning alters the very experience of reality for the individual. Psychosis is thus characterized as a form of *perceptual distress*, a significant change in the qualitative aspects of cognitive processing that gives rise to an altered experience of reality. This approach also incorporates an explicit acknowledgement of the metacognitive nature of the experience.

This cognitive model is in some respects anchored in empirical evidence inasmuch as there is a range of cognitive psychological research that demonstrates that individuals with a diagnosis of psychosis exhibit a number of identifiable differences in the nature of their thinking (Frith, 1992; Garety and Freeman, 1999; Broome et al., 2007). I would argue that the definition of psychosis provided by the RCP is misleading in that it fails to draw upon the distinction that our experience of reality is individually and socially constructed (Berger and Luckmann, 1966). The contribution of social and personal construction to our experience of reality is evident empirically in a diverse range of social science disciplines and particularly in cognitive science.

What is recovery?

The idea of recovery is no less fraught with controversy than the understanding of what the person is endeavouring to recover from (or in relation to). In the last 20 years, the UK has seen a rise in the idea of recovery as an emerging alternative paradigm for understanding mental illness. Recovery emerged from the grass roots of the consumer/survivor movement during the latter part of the 1980s and early 1990s, particularly in the United States (Shepherd et al., 2008). It has entered into the professional domain and is now at a point where recovery, or perhaps more accurately a professionally embraced interpretation thereof, is beginning to influence the creation of top-down governmental policy [Department of Health (DOH), 2009, 2011].

Typically, the professional mental health literature contrasts the ideas of personal recovery with those of clinical recovery. Clinical recovery is pitched as the medical view of symptoms going into remission and/or being 'managed' by treatment – typically by means of medication (Slade, 2009). Personal recovery, in contrast, is seen as living well and fruitfully in spite of or in the face of continued difficulties with so-called mental health problems (Slade, 2009). The most widely cited definition is that of Anthony (1993, p. 17):

> Recovery is a deeply personal, unique process of changing one's attitudes, values, feelings, goals, skills, and/or roles. It is a way of living a satisfying, hopeful, and contributing life even within the limitations caused by illness. Recovery involves the development of new meaning and purpose in one's life as one grows beyond the catastrophic effects of mental illness.

So, recovery originated from service-user/consumer/survivor accounts of how mental illness can be overcome and, to some extent or other, recovered from. Some of these hopeful stories or narratives emphasize how life can be worthwhile in the face of mental illness, and there are yet others expressing ideas of complete recovery. Perhaps it is better to think of self-discovery or self-transformation as a key component of these stories rather than 'recovery from' a mental health difficulty. An argument against recovery that was presented at a recent international refocus on recovery conference was that it is still too closely tied to medicine and entails a belief that there is 'something wrong with the person' that necessitates recovery (Beresford, 2012). The present literature on personal recovery indeed presents a partial recovery picture or one in which the recovery is centered around not so much the resolution of the 'illness defined' portion of the person's functioning as those other areas of life that are initially obstructed or impaired because of the arrival of 'mental illness'.

A LIVED EXPERIENCE PERSPECTIVE ON RECOVERY

My own recovery from psychosis was one that took at least five years from the last active experience of persistent unusual beliefs and thoughts. I present my recovery journey, what that was like and how I reached a point of complete recovery in subsequent chapters. I certainly agree with the idea of recovery being a personalized 'journey' and that it has a stage-like quality (Andresen et al., 2003). The borders/boundaries of those stages are, from my experience, pretty fuzzy, and it's possible to slip back and forth between the stages (vacillate) over time, and it takes time to settle within a stage. (In some senses, I liken the experience of moving between stages as being similar to Piaget's (1964) conception of stages of cognitive development in that there are processes of equilibrium and disequilibrium at work.)

It can be tough, when you are alone in your recovery, to distinguish where you are in the stages, and some stages can zip by a lot faster than others. Reaching a stage of growth and realizing with confidence that you have reached this point is in my experience something that takes the most amount of time in recovering from psychosis. Having confidence in your relatively newly acquired resilience (i.e. the capacity to withstand distress without relapse or collapse) takes time to develop and requires the experience of stabilization in your recovery and successfully testing your capacity to withstand distress. I believe also that the idea of personal recovery, as currently espoused within the recovery literature, presents one possible outcome. It is not the only possible outcome of a recovery journey. I think also that not all aspire or can reach complete recovery; some settle for personal recovery or can obtain it 'only' in the sense that it is currently being used in the literature. Others yet, for a host of reasons, find themselves at the protracted mercy of their condition and rightly may find the idea of recovery, particularly if insensitively delivered, as offensive and invalidating.

I find some of the ideas inherent in the definitions in personal recovery so far presented to be insufficient to capture the diversity of recovery trajectories. That complete recovery from a personal perspective, in contrast to and along the spectrum of clinical recovery, is not raised is a serious concern to me. Clinical recovery is the gloomiest prospect of recovery to me. The idea of having an underlying or dormant illness that can relapse at any given moment is not a hopeful state of being. Personal recovery with still a component of living with the difficulties imposed by mental illness is similarly gloomy to me, although it is a reality for many. The ideas of how recovery can be best achieved and the ideas of recovery-oriented practice are, however, ones that I can get alongside. The ideas of promoting and developing the well-being of individuals struggling with their mental health also resonate strongly and positively with me. A focus on things outside the rituals of treatment that can promote improvement also feels like a particularly significant shift.

I made the most substantive steps in my recovery *after* I'd left professional mental health services. This was because the central preoccupation of the service was in treating what they saw as my illness without working meaningfully on those other areas of my life that were put on hold as a result of this – namely, my living circumstances and prospects for returning to work and employment. Many of the faltering steps I made subsequently were, in hindsight, ones that improved my well-being, self-identity and sense of satisfaction with life (Leamy et al., 2011).

What are the potential benefits of recovery-oriented practice?

A shift towards a recovery-oriented picture for service delivery provokes mental health services to change its work in supporting individuals who use the service. Traditionally mental health services are geared to provide treatment for people with mental illnesses; they are 'mental illness services' first and foremost (Anthony, 1993). The spotlight is on the illness and on how best to work with that, resolve it or minimize its impact on the person's ability to function. With a recovery orientation, the focus moves towards how the person's life and well-being can best be supported, maintained and improved, at the same time providing treatment for the person's difficulties. This is not a trivial shifting of the goalposts; there is simply a broader focus and recognition of needing to emphasize improving well-being with the recovery orientation.

I would therefore find myself in agreement with Mapplebeck (2010) in arguing for a reconsideration of psychosis in relation to recovery as one of 'post-traumatic growth'. There is a growing body of research that supports this reframing. Some of this is evident from the emerging findings that there is a high 'co-morbidity' of individuals with psychosis *and* post-traumatic stress disorder (PTSD) (Bogár and Perczel, 2007; Chisholm et al., 2006). The relationship between psychosis and PTSD has been theorized as comprising three kinds: that traumatic life events trigger psychosis, that psychosis is in itself a traumatic experience that leads in turn to PTSD and that perhaps they are both best thought of as a continuum of responses to traumatic events and that both PTSD and psychosis are part of the same spectrum (Morrison et al., 2003).

It is possible, then, that we could do away with the term 'psychosis' (and diagnoses such as schizophrenia) and instead talk about distressing, unwanted and unusual trauma-related experiences, where that description is relevant to the person at hand (not all unusual experiences *are* unwanted). Whilst this is not as pithy as 'psychosis', it gets a bit closer to the experience and, with added personalization, can embrace more meaning. It can also perhaps help to detach the person from unhelpful stigmatizing labels such as schizo, psycho and the like.

Recovery, psychosis and mental health nursing

It's worth reflecting here upon how these issues – in how terms like 'psychosis' and 'recovery' are constructed and understood – impact upon mental health nursing practice. In the most recent revision of the NMC (Nursing and Midwifery Council) practice standards, mental health nurses are directed, in terms of their professional values, to "work in a way that promotes positive relationships focused on social inclusion, human rights and recovery, that is, a person's ability to live a self-directed life, with or without symptoms, that they believe is meaningful and satisfying" (Goodman and Ley, 2012, p. 157; NMC, 2010). Here clearly there is an attempt to embrace the ideas of personal recovery, and it is interesting that the standard just quoted expands beyond Anthony's (1993) definition of personal recovery and is neutral with respect to the experience of symptoms.

It is also noticeable that the NMC standards in relation to nursing practice commends mental health nurses to "draw on a range of evidence-based psychological, psychosocial and other complex therapeutic skills and interventions to provide person-centred support and care across all ages, in a way that supports self-determination and aids recovery" (Goodman and Ley, 2012, p. 157; NMC, 2010). Given that the rise of recovery-oriented practice in part constitutes an emerging paradigm shift in conceptualizing what the focus of mental health services should be. A parallel consequence is that it also serves to galvanize research in the field of mental health to develop valid mixed-method approaches in research that raise the profile and standing of lived experience as a source of evidence.

There is an intrinsic problem here with regard to what we mean by 'evidenced-based'. This again is not a neutral (value-free) territory. What constitutes good-quality evidence is subject to dominance within the fields of research, academic and clinical practice; a great deal is at stake. Grant (2009) sums up some of the largely unvoiced tensions in speaking about what constitutes evidence-based practice in cognitive-behavioural therapy (CBT), the dominant form of psychotherapy in the UK (Andersson et al., 2005). Grant points to the work of Salkovskis (2002), who flags the limitations of taking too narrow an approach to evidence-based practice – namely, where there is a preoccupation with RCTs (randomized controlled trials), meta-analyses and systematic reviews – as the gold-standard of research evidence. Grant (2009) pushes for an approach to research evidence that takes its cue from the post-modern, that is being critical of political power attached to 'accepted wisdom', and that embraces more qualitative/interpretative methodologies. The problem with applying the principles of natural science (e.g. positivism and reductionism) to human sciences is that seeking to objectify the person can result in wringing all the relevant meaning out of their experience. Yet we must learn from the limitations of so-called introspectionism. It's clear that evidence-based or informed practice needs to draw upon and synthesize what can be learned from empiricism – where specific hypotheses can be tested and generalities inferred, in addition to the intricate, rich detail afforded by qualitative research and lived experience.

Mental health professionals as a whole, then, should strive to understand where recovery has come from and how it seeks to change how services are delivered. The shift is not away from treatment for all but rather towards mental health professionals' getting serious about working to actively promote 'mental health', rather than being solely preoccupied with working only with the symptoms of 'mental illness'. Understanding the nuances and ramifications of this shift, especially within the embedded contexts, is vital for nursing and allied professions to develop the more collaborative, coaching-style role recommended for recovery-oriented practice (Slade, 2009).

An introduction to post-modernism in mental health

In Grant's (2009) call for a 'paradigmatic pluralism', alluded to earlier, we are witnessing the impact of so-called post-modernity to the field of mental health. Post-modernism is, by nature, a notoriously slippery concept to address. It's hard even to be certain that 'concept' is an appropriate word to use! Post-modernity as a strand of socially critical thinking has emerged, as the name implies, to challenge the orthodoxy and legitimacy of modernist approaches. In the context of mental health, this includes the current insistence in medicine, nursing and psychiatry *that science should necessarily be our sole guide* in clinical practice (Bracken and Thomas, 2001). Western culture is, amongst many other things, dominated by rationality and individualism (see for example the work of Brooks, 2012, and Dawkins, 2011). It has legitimized technical expertise as a means for treating 'mental ill-health', evident in the rise of psychiatry, psychology and psychotherapy as *professional disciplines* and the Mental Health Act (1983/2007) as a means of legislating, enforcing and policing aspects of practice.

Post-modernism seeks to highlight the importance of *context* to our understanding of mental health difficulties. It does not seek to discard empirical knowledge but rather to recognize that historical and cultural rules proscribe how we gain access to and disseminate truth (O'Farrell, 2006). In this sense, I would argue that the so-called recovery movement is a reflection of both anti-psychiatry and post-psychiatry reactions to mental health services and culture. It is itself vulnerable to inadvertent co-option into the 'mainstream' mental health agenda, and there have been concerns particularly amongst service-user and survivor groups that the current politicization and professional adoption of recovery represent little more than just this (Davidson et al., 2006).

It is worth noting that post-modernism is not itself without criticism – take for example the seminal work of Sokal (1996), who conducted an experiment to demonstrate that science is vulnerable to 'abuse' under the banner of post-modernity. Sokal undertook a hoax – by writing a parody of a post-modernist–style physics paper and seeing whether it would get published in one of the leading cultural studies journals. It was, and this fueled their subsequent critique that, when mishandled, post-modernism lends itself to the abuse of natural sciences (Sokal, 1996).

Bearing all this in mind, this volume will present a 'sceptical post-modernist' account of the current state of empirically supported evidence on recovering from psychosis. In doing so, I am arguing for the adoption of an approach to thinking that aims for what I call 'the proper treatment of Foucault'. Foucault is, of course, a writer to whom a significant chunk of post-modernity is attributed – one of the founders, if you will, of the post-modernist movement. At the heart of this agenda is the recognition that it is a potentially catastrophic misconception that 'things acquire reality' as a result of *social practices alone*. Rather, it promotes the idea that Foucault was exploring the consequences of the apprehension of the 'raw' through a myriad of cultural and conceptual mechanisms that are both complex and dictated to by our particular historical and cultural setting (O'Farrell, 2006).

What do we gain from favouring a sceptical post-modernist account? First, we are afforded both leverage and a means to challenge the dominance of more psychopathological accounts of people with mental illnesses. One way in which this is achieved is through being able to constructively challenge the validity of the kinds of evidence and research methods that are seen as legitimate in clinical practice, education and research. Second, and most tellingly, the post-modernist account seeks to broaden our understanding of how our own cultural practices can distort the validity and truth value of our knowledge. Third, some psychotherapeutic approaches have embraced aspects of post-modernist thought (e.g. Narrative Therapy and some variations derived from Cognitive-Behavioural Therapy, such as Acceptance and Commitment Therapy) into their therapeutic methods, and this had led to new ways of thinking about and working with people with SMIs.

Post-post modernism or trans-modernism

Insofar as it relates meaningfully to mental health, the approach related to trans-modernism will be applied as an alternative critical framework (Dussel, 1995). This is particularly relevant because trans-modernism, as espoused by Dussel but also evident in the developing 'liberation psychologies', adopts a "critical perspective of the oppressed other" (Burton and Osorio, 2011, p. 23). Dussel argues, from his wide-ranging philosophical and ethical exploration of political movements in Latin America, that to liberate people from exploitation necessitates a reaching out with parity to those who are at the fringes of or outside the system (Dussel, 1995). In the mental health context, this in some senses could be likened to aspects of recovery-oriented research where there is a vested interest in researching with people who have avoided or escaped engagement in the mental health treatment system and who nonetheless have learned to flourish in their lives. They have somehow addressed their emotional and sociopsychological needs successfully without or in spite of the system's attempts to 'support' (Coleman, 1999). This also maps onto the movement to embrace peer professionals with lived experience as part of the Department of Health's (DOH, 2001) early vision for mental health care recovery-focused services.

Can recovery happen for people with a diagnosis of psychosis?

Irrespective of how we should think about psychosis and what it is, an important question to answer is whether recovery can happen. Whilst it's arguably crucially important to clarify precisely what is happening in the processes of psychoses so that we can work more effectively with those who experience them, it is both clinically and pragmatically vital to convey an appropriately hopeful message for people's future. People can and do recover fully from severe experiences of psychosis that are diagnosed as schizophrenia. People have 'episodes' or 'bouts', recover, and never experience them again. Others' experiences of psychosis are more recurrent and persistent, and some persons appear to have to learn to live with the condition, learn to cope with it as it fluctuates in intensity and aim to thrive in their lives in spite of it.

The evidence for this can be found in the existing research literature in the half-dozen or so long-term follow-up studies of psychosis. The emerging picture from these studies is that the tenacious assumption that conditions such as schizophrenia are necessarily chronic, deteriorating diseases is not supported by empirical evidence and equates to a clinical myth. Without needing our post-modernist tools to criticize the legitimacy of this kind of knowledge, it is already evident within the confines of outcome-based research that the 'clinical rule of thirds – a third recover, a third have a relapsing-remitting course and a third never get better and get worse' is palpably untrue. Harding and colleagues' (1987) longitudinal study alone, with a 32-year follow-up period, establishes that, overall, 81% of the participating sample described themselves as independent, and 68% described themselves as having 'moderately close' relationships. Only 11% of the overall sample were left struggling significantly with their experiences and needing sustained service support. The reality of this data and those of other studies is a much more optimistic (and spectrum-like) picture for the trajectory and development of the lifespan of these emotional and psychological experiences.

In addition to this body of empirical evidence, we have an increasing presence of service-user and survivor accounts of recovery that are filtering back into clinical practice via the professional domain (e.g. influential authors such as Patricia Deegan and Ron Coleman). Recovered service-users are entering the professional and clinical domains that inform education, research and clinical practice. There is an increasing trend in National Health Service (NHS) mental health services to recruit positively for professionals with lived experience, and alongside this there are practice developments and innovations that employ experts-by-experience as peer professionals (Slade, 2012). This marks an infusion of the 'other' into the system that, as Dussel would put it, forms a growing 'interpellation' – where the voices and views of the needs of those formally harmed, not helped by or marginalized by their experiences of services and the surrounding legal-bureaucratic systems (e.g. welfare benefits) are being heard and recognized by traditional services within (Repper and Carter, 2011).

Conclusions

Summing up, the development of mental health practice is currently experiencing what we might consider to be 'interesting times' (Coudert, 1939; Buchanan, 2013). Psychiatry is under increasing external and internal scrutiny in terms of its scientific and professional legitimacy (Bracken and Thomas, 2001). New approaches to talking about and working with the psychoses are demanded by the insufficiency of traditional practice as the NHS manoeuvres irrevocably to services that demonstrate effectiveness transparently and as a means to justify continued financing (Health and Social Care Act, 2012). The urgency for this has been fuelled by our current austere economic climate in the UK, which is leading to sustained organizational restructuring (Health and Social Care Act, 2012). These political, philosophical and pragmatic pressures appear to be combining to serve to make the shift towards a recovery-oriented form of practice particularly attractive.

Recovery ostensibly has emerged from survivor roots but is now inevitably engaged in a professional reinterpretation. It is thus vulnerable to the vicissitudes of any developing competing master narrative (Bakhtin, 1981). A positive consequence of this shift is the emergence of the desire to create values-based, collaborative, person-centred, well-being-oriented strands of mental health services. The realization of this organizational dream is unlikely to be unproblematic, however; there will be forms of organizational resistance, dilution or what we could collectively refer to as 'transformational difficulties' (Slade, 2009, 2012).

A post-modern account of psychosis demands a retelling. Emerging research evidence suggests credibility for aligning it with an experience on the 'trauma spectrum' (Morrison et al., 2003). Mental health nursing, amongst the milieu of mental health professionals in the UK, is prominently placed as a potential key professional body in the adoption of recovery-oriented practice and, I would argue, would do well to embrace a paradigmatically pluralistic, post-modernist stance with respect to evidence and formulating working practices (Grant, 2009). Irrespective of how appropriate 'recovery' is as an umbrella term for practice, education and research change, there is no doubt that it already happens for people with psychosis and SMI. At the moment, it has been politically embraced and is positioned to make a lasting and positive effect on the development of mental health services and culture.

Chapter 3

An autoethnographic account of psychosis in the context of neurobiological, cognitive psychological and meta-synthetic analysis

This chapter provides an account of what can happen to a person during the immediate emergence of experiencing a 'psychosis'. It draws upon the author's lived experience and provides a first-person account. Interwoven with this account, a detailed review of current meta-synthetic, cognitive, medical and neurobiological models of psychosis will be provided. Wherever possible, the author's experience will be used to illustrate key points of the respective models. The models and literature will also be explored, where relevant, with an eye to a post-modern critical constructivist, trans-modernist and evidence-based perspective.

BACKGROUND OF MY LIVED EXPERIENCE

My difficulties with psychosis emerged shortly after completing my bachelor's of science degree in experimental psychology at the University of Sussex. To my way of thinking, both personally and professionally as a nurse, nurse-therapist and psychologist, the precursors of my later adult psychological traumatic experiences (that otherwise can be termed 'psychoses') are to be found in my formative and childhood years. I am also persuaded by the idea that certain biological vulnerabilities exist that also contribute to the unfolding of a person's psychological make-up and experiences. I would couch this within an interactionist stress-vulnerability model of psychosocial development (Zubin and Spring, 1977). I completed my bachelor's degree in 2001 and obtained the only first-class award for my cohort that year. It marked the completion of three years of mostly hard, sustained effort. I was so painfully self-effacing at the time that I was pretty much the only person in my class who didn't think I was going to get a first! I was very surprised and pleased, and I can remember being called in for an interview, not because I was on the borders of the classification for my degree, which is the normal purpose for an interview, but because the department wanted to discuss my future prospects as an academic and a psychologist! I was pretty clear that I wanted to continue, and I was encouraged to pursue a postgraduate qualification – that is, a doctorate and within the department, too.

Flushed with academic success, I had my first experience of living away from home around this time and my first, even by my own standards, awkward experiences of personal relationships as well. I grew up in a tiny hamlet (not even a village) on a farm in Sussex, part of a close-knit community (in some senses) in which everyone pretty much knew everything about what everybody else was doing by virtue of its miniscule size. I recall there being an announcement of my academic success in the parish magazine, along with a statement of my intention to study 'computational psychology' at the University of Sussex for a PhD. For me, it felt as though my wishes and dreams were coming true, and this had, I suppose in retrospect, a somewhat surreal edge. Some authors with more medical perspective on psychosis speak of a 'prodromal mood', and perhaps on reflection this was the beginning of what could be described as such for me, insofar as the concept of a prodrome can be considered relevant to a more psychogenic account of psychosis (Woods et al., 2009). No one else I knew of in my family had managed to get a degree, although I recall a cousin of mine also gained a qualification in pursuit of her veterinary science career, and she may have beaten me to the punch. This was no small thing for the son of a farm labourer and care worker.

It was at the end of my first year of doctoral studies that serious difficulties with my mental health emerged. I was a slow starter emotionally and socially. I had quite a few friends socially outside of university, but not really a very wide network and not a great deal of self-confidence in my early twenties. I didn't have much 'common' sense, as my family and schoolmates seemed fond of pointing out to me. I poured my energies into my studies and the pursuit of academic qualifications. Part of this, I think on reflection, was to avoid engaging with my home life. Until my first doctorate attempt (I'm in the throes of considering doing this again at the tender age of 43), I'd pretty much ever known only academic success. I'd passed all my O levels, and it was only when I took A-level chemistry and S-level biology that I had some academic failure.

EXPERIENCING ABUSE AND TRAUMA

I was unfortunate enough as life unfolded to encounter an ongoing number of types of traumatic experience. I was bullied repeatedly at times in the latter part of school – the fifth and sixth forms. I recall one incident where another kid at school (and this is secondary school, so I was a teenager at the time), sat on me in a bus stop and wouldn't let me get up to catch my bus. At the same time, he stuffed pictures from pornographic magazines into my coat, jumper and school bag. This kid victimized me on and off repeatedly as I went through school. These were such humiliating and painful experiences at the time that I never felt able to tell anyone about them in any systematic or helpful way. I couldn't process them emotionally on my own either. Another bully at school tried setting fire to my trousers once. I recall being locked in a school locker as another incident (which didn't help my confidence much) and also having to endure being teased sexually by some pretty aggressive girls in the school. So adolescence was from my point of view rather fraught and harrowing at times. It seemed to me also that the world was a cruel, nasty and vicious place and that I couldn't immediately find somebody to help guide me.

As I think over my formative years just from a school life point of view, I can go on and on reeling out unhappy experiences of being bullied and victimized largely from an emotional standpoint as a kind of abuse. There were some experiences of deprivation and physical abuses too. Along this spectrum, there were several instances of different kinds of sexually related abuse. These are the most painful and difficult to contemplate. Whilst now I can think and talk about these things with relative clarity and without, most of the time, particularly overwhelming negative emotional reactions, they remain things that I prefer not to disclose in detail for obvious reasons. It is, I think, sufficient to say, stepping for a moment out of my story again, that there is increasingly robust empirical evidence that people with an experience of psychosis often have experience of abuse in their childhood and adult lives. It's worth reviewing this at this point to gain some wider evidential context.

A relatively recent and significant literature review by Read and colleagues (2005) established that "there is now substantial evidence linking child sexual abuse (CSA) and child physical abuse (CPA) to a range of mental health problems *in childhood*" (p. 331, emphasis added). It was not until 2004 that research specifically into the possible causal role of experiences of trauma for psychosis really took off. Prior to that, the idea of some kind of trauma or abuse having a role to play in the unfolding of unusual experiences labelled as psychosis was not commonplace in psychiatry. To this day, there remains a considerable amount of inertia against these ideas. It also seems to be that lately in psychological research the idea of causality has become something of a dirty word in favour of less powerful (or more indirect) concepts of moderating and mediating factors. Read and colleagues' (2005) review remains, however, a particularly key point of our knowledge development. Read and fellows (2005) acknowledge that whilst post-childhood trauma is a possible mediating factor for (something that sits between and contributes to the development of) psychosis, it was not the immediate focus of their review. A confounding factor for the literature in teasing out the role of trauma is that diagnoses of post-traumatic stress disorder (PTSD) are often made and given precedence to diagnoses relating to psychoses in individuals who report trauma experiences. Indeed, this is what we would expect and hope in terms of pitching psychosis as part of the trauma/confusion spectrum.

In Read and colleagues' (2005) review, the finding is that *most* 'psychiatric patients' (and here I cannot help but encase this term in single scare-quotes) suffer serious physical assaults in adulthood. This is corroborated by Cascardi and fellows' (1996) study that found that in the year before admission to hospital, 63% had suffered physical violence by their partners, and 46% of those living at home had been assaulted by family members. Problems of how reliable self-report is in 'this population' are often raised but are not empirically validated. For those diagnosed with psychoses, doubt is often cast clinically and in the media upon the reliability of their reports and/or accusations. Research specifically in this area indicates that actually such reports of abuse are in fact reliable, and for instance in terms of finding confirmatory evidence for reports of CSA, this has been found in 74% and 82% of cases (Herman and Schatzow, 1987; Read et al., 2005). Typically, people actually under-report such instances (Dill et al., 1991). This clinical bias is particularly poignant from my own experience of inpatient care and is one that I am particularly keen as a nurse-educator to address with mental health professionals currently in training. I recall once disclosing my experiences of abuse and trauma to a staff nurse, who told me that she couldn't talk to me about that right now. That was the last time I talked about it whilst an inpatient; it was never addressed again.

HOW MY PSYCHOSIS EMERGED

In the run-up to the emergence of 'strange' thoughts, beliefs and actions, I was engaged in my first year of doctoral studies. I use the term 'strange' here with some reservations. They were certainly strange-sounding to others when I gave voice to them during the limited opportunities I had to discuss what was going on in my head. They were also at times, although not always, strange to me as well. Sometimes I accepted them as they were – almost akin to how you don't question the odd things that happen when you are dreaming. There is little doubt in my mind, from a purely experiential perspective, that there are disturbances to the degree of conscious awareness you have whilst in so-called psychotic states. So, at this time, I had three PhD supervisors, with different expertises and backgrounds. Anybody who has studied at this level, as well as those who have not, will perhaps readily grasp the idea (and once again I appreciate that this is with the benefit of hindsight) that this was not such a good plan, even though it was well intended as I was pursuing essentially an interdisciplinary topic and approach. However, it meant that conflicting points of view and competing demands were presented to me. None of these things, I would say, solely stood over the other as a causal factor: psychosis is a multi-factorial beast.

My studies entailed a lot of solitary study, reading and working with computer programming approaches. This meant a lot of solo work poring over the minutiae of the program and the infuriating pursuit of bugs in the software. Also, the best time to run my programs, in order to get the best out of the mainframe, was in the evening and overnight. Later on, it was a mechanism for avoiding others when I was more depressed and struggling to get back into my doctoral studies. Initially, though, I ended up working a-social hours. Sleep deprivation ensued and also limited contact with peers, colleagues, friends and family. The typical young male inexperience of self-care, my past formative experience and a history of mental ill health in my family made for a classic mix for potential severe mental health difficulties (Zubin and Spring, 1977).

One snag (or benefit, depending on your point of view) of the experience of psychosis is that it's often hard to recall what happened. The same can be said of recall in trauma (Ehlers and Clark, 2000), and an advantage of placing psychosis within a spectrum of trauma is that the same neurophysiological mechanisms that putatively underpin post-traumatic stress and mediate poor declarative memory formation can theoretically be co-opted into filling in some of the gaps of the story of psychosis. I'm a relatively poor historian anyway, I think, and there are definite gaps in my memory of these times. This is hardly surprising as the overall picture of memory research in psychosis tells us that there are significant problems with episodic and long-term memory, whilst short-term, implicit and procedural memory appears to be relatively unaffected (Berrios and Hodges, 2000). Also from a neurobiological perspective, what we know of trauma and memory arguably fits this picture. The work of Schiller and contemporaries on the nature of memory supports the idea that our memories are a kind of ongoing notation to the self or 'narrative construct' of how our past relates to the present (Schiller et al., 2010).

What I can say is that I can recall the day when everything changed for me like a paradigm shift of experience (i.e. the world around me seemed to change), and I ended up admitted to an acute mental health unit. It was my relationship to self, the world and others and how this affected my actions that ultimately led to my admission. To this end, I support taking a 'relational frame view' of our psychological experiences (Hayes, 2004). I was frazzled and had been puzzling over a particularly thorny problem with my work. I needed to consult with someone about the problems I was wrestling with. I recall lurching out of my dungeon of an office beset with the task of finding somebody in the department who could help me with my problem. I felt driven and on a mission, so to speak. The few people I thought would be able to help I couldn't find, and I recall bumping into people in the corridor, common room and department library, asking them if they'd seen such and such a person.

Frustration grew as I failed to find anybody helpful. I went round in circles and was frustrated. I started to wonder why I couldn't find the help I needed and where these people were. At this point, I think my thinking started to unravel and become increasingly tenuous, as though I was working through a decreasingly probable list of reasons for my failure to find the person. I started to lose touch with the reason for my frustration and was absorbed into the emotion of feeling 'on the hunt', driven and at times perplexed. It's key to understand that, in the onset of psychosis, emotional experiences and drives are happening. A drive to understand your own experience and explain it to yourself – particularly when it's becoming increasingly at odds with others and the world about you – that can, I think, accelerate the person into even more bizarre spirals of experience. This would fit with Dennett's work (1991) on the 'intentionalist stance', that is, recognizing that much of our conscious experience is from the perspective of understanding our own intentions (why we are doing things), as well as others' (the so-called theory of mind problem).

From these relatively benign beginnings, my mind spiralled out of apparent control, thinking with wilder and wilder thoughts about what was going on. I was well used to thinking up alternatives and listening to my thoughts; years of practice in analogical reasoning came, I would say readily, to my destruction. Other emotions started to emerge. Some undertones of hopelessness. A developing sense that I was alone (a frequent reality in undertaking postgraduate work) but at this time magnified to an excruciatingly uncomfortable and palpable degree. This was a pain-laden experience. This is a point of emphasis for me – these kinds of experiences can invoke strong, bodily felt sensations that are hard for the individual to account for, and, in working with them, exploring felt sensations in the body is vital in my opinion.

McCarthy-Jones and colleagues' (2013) recently published meta-synthesis of qualitative research into people's experiences of psychosis tells us that one common theme in this experience for people is one of 'losing'. This is a loss not entirely akin to 'depression', although it has some clear commonalities. It includes a loss of 'consensual reality'. There is a despairingly sad, isolationist quality to these losses as within this theme are a 'loss of self', 'loss of help and motivation', 'loss of relationships', 'pain', as well as a second group of themes that converge around a need for help to 're-build and reforge' as a result.

I recall fleeting moments of rushing across the university campus, seeing posters on the walls that seemed to speak only to me. From a bio-psychiatric perspective, this is termed 'ideas of reference'. In some ways, as my thoughts accelerated so did I, as I was physically seeking out and picking up on 'clues'. I would relate this acceleration to being semantically and semiotically driven from a cognitive-psychological perspective. It is also worth pointing out that a recent, more bio-psychiatric framework for understanding psychosis is that of 'aberrant salience' wherein a putative role of the neurochemical dopamine is in mediating the experience of 'salience' (Kapur, 2003). Dopamine is a neurochemical heavily implicated in psychoses by virtue of the primary pharmacological action of antipsychotic drugs. This had become something now of a quest, and I can vividly recall when I sat in the police cell, a place of safety, having marched in of my own accord, that I was on some heaven-sent mission. This is particularly ironic, given my now staunchly polite anti-theistic and atheistic views.

What does cognitive science have to say about this?

In terms of cognitive models of psychosis, there is a largely conflicting mass of micro theories, particularly as they relate to cognitive-behavioural therapies for psychosis. It's worth saying at this point that there is to my mind a considerable distance in the cutting edge of cognitive science and the application of its psychotherapeutic cousin (see the seminal and still relevant Bieling and Kuyken, 2003). To stretch the metaphor a little further, these are distant cousins at least several times removed. Whereas Beck's cognitive-behavioural therapy for anxiety or depression revolves around a coherent theme of emotions – namely, fear and loss for the two conditions – the current cognitive-behavioural theories that underpin CBT for psychosis do not have such a basis (Grant et al., 2010).

I tend therefore to find myself still in agreement with Birchwood and Trower's (2006) concerns that whilst some hope is emerging from research findings that psychotherapy can become a credible treatment for psychosis, the idea that it must adhere to a 'quasi-neuroleptic' metaphor is problematic. In spite of mid-twentieth-century psychiatry's concerted attempt, helmed by Jaspers (1962, cited in Birchwood and Trower, 2006), to cast psychosis asunder from emotion, the developing consensus of twenty-first-century research is that this is a relationship that needs saving, with conciliatory and reformatory talks well underway.

A neat summary of the state of these various macro and micro theories can be found in Fletcher and Frith's (2009) cogent review of cognitive theories. A word of caution, courtesy of post-modernism, though: these theories still tell their story of psychosis heavily underwritten by neuroscience and with an appeal to the language of logically positivistic biological psychiatry. Some theories hold that experiences, couched by psychiatry as delusions and hallucinations, are kinds of 'abnormal perceptions'. The theories that take this path are typically in two stages. First, the person has to have some kind of disturbed, anomalous sensory experience (hallucinations). Delusions then follow on from this as a result of trying to make sense of the first troubling experience. These kinds of theory have been around at least since the mid-1970s and are exemplified by the likes of Maher (1974, cited in Fletcher and Frith, 2009).

In this vein, there are also theories such as Kapur's (2003) that attempt to conjoin biology, pharmacology and phenomenology by positing that what underlies conditions such as schizophrenia within the umbrella of psychosis is a matter of problems of 'aberrant salience' underpinned by slow neurochemical modulation (Corlett et al., 2009). What this means is that the person pays too much scrutiny to stimuli in the world that have little or no import. Another variant theory of this kind is that not self-monitoring sufficiently well causes the 'positive' signs of psychosis (Lindner et al., 2005). These kinds of explanations seem best placed to explain the more 'passive' aspects of psychosis, according to Fletcher and Frith (2009)'s review, but struggle in the face of more active experiences such as delusions.

Supporting evidence for the aberrant salience hypothesis comes from what little work exists on computational models of brain processes. Grasemann and colleagues (2010) simulated the effects of aberrant salience on a neural network of story understanding and recall. Neural networks are a kind of computational model revived in the late 1980s that is inspired by animal neurons (Gurney, 1997). They are mathematical models of neuron-like 'units' whose ability to process information is dependent on the many interconnections between them (Gurney, 1997). In Grasemann and colleagues' (2010) simulation, a network was given all of the components of stories to learn (coded into a set of patterns), and the effects of different kinds of manipulations to the network's functioning was analyzed by looking at how the networked functioned after the lesioning (i.e. different kinds of change applied to the network). One manipulation involved using 'high learning rates' (hyperlearning) to make the network's attention to environmental information distorted in the manner proposed by Kapur (2003). In analyzing the output of these networks, they found stable patterns of 'agency shifts', where characters in the stories moved between stories, producing new meaningful narratives and where agency shifts often involved the 'self'. Also amongst these shifts of agency were examples of 'derailments' – where the language produced by the network becomes disorganized and unable to pursue a coherent narrative thread. This kind of theoretical and computational work provides support for developing interventions that target neurocognitive functioning – for example cognitive remediation therapy (see Chapter 4).

Some cognitive theories are more micro than others. Morrison (2001) proposes that both hallucinations and delusions are kinds of 'intrusion' and that it is the interpretation of these that leads people to struggle and encounter distress. This aligns psychosis, as a kind of experience akin to the relatively well developed cognitive models of obsessions and compulsions (à la Salkovskis et al., 1995), and a metacognitive approach that has had some success also in treating OCD (obsessive compulsive disorder) (Wells and Papageorgiou, 1998). Part of the difficulty that cognitive models of psychosis have had, in the UK in particular, is that they tend to be extensions or adaptations of previously existing cognitive models of emotional difficulties rather than starting from a fresh position.

Bentall and colleagues (1994) have developed a strand of research into psychosis that emphasizes a functional rather than a dysfunctional role for paranoid styles of thinking. They argue that it protects self-esteem by minimizing opportunities to realize the gaps between the actual and ideal selves. Studies by this group have found some support for a bias towards external attribution and negative self-concepts that adds credence to this hypothesis. Jumping-to-conclusions research is a strand of well-replicated research that supports this line of thinking (Garety et al., 1991). The participant in these kinds of study is typically presented with various pots of different coloured balls – for example blue and red with an 80-to-20% ratio. In these controlled experiments, people with delusions are quicker than those without such reported experiences to choose which of the containers that a sequence of balls drawn out and presented to them has come from. In addition, they are more confident about the accuracy of these decisions (Garety et al., 1991).

An enduring psychological account of the problems that feature in psychosis is the theory of mind deficit (Frith, 1992). In this model, a central dysfunction in the ability to represent the mental state of others and to distinguish this from one's own mental state is posited. This model holds that this failure arises because of a dysfunction with 'meta-representational' processes (McCabe et al., 2004). Meta-representation, put simply, is the ability to have beliefs and thoughts about our thoughts. In a meta-representational failure, it is believed that something disrupts the links between the initial thought (or primary representation) and the thought about that thought (secondary representation) (McCabe et al., 2004). More concretely, say John has a thought ('I have my appointment tomorrow') and then has a subsequent thought about that ('Oh yes, Bill told me I should attend my appointment, it's important'). If there is a meta-representational failure – perhaps part of the representation is distorted or mislabelled – then it's possible that rather than recalling the secondary representation as being a memory of something Bill told John, it could instead be perceived as a voice-like command saying, 'You should attend your appointment tomorrow', no longer attached or labelled as a memory of something Bill once said or specifically belonging to John himself. This would be experienced as an intrusive thought that seemed to be put into John's mind or as a voice-like experience as John reflects upon the nature of that experience.

In other words, a voice-hearing experience could be understood as a kind of meta-representational, contextual labelling malfunction. This is very similar to Perner's developmental 'fading context marker hypothesis' for representational modelling errors that occur in children's normative cognitive development (Perner, 1991). The implication here is that the kinds of cognitive processes that are at fault in the development of psychosis in adulthood are mirrors to errors that arise in regular cognitive development in childhood in a different contextual domain. Indeed, McKay and Dennett (2009), in their lengthy philosophical analysis of misbelief, suggest that so-called delusions may serve a protective adaptive function (the so-called doxastic shear pin hypothesis). This is partially borne out by the evidence supporting Bentall and colleagues' (1994) self-esteem protection hypothesis and the parallels between Perner's (1991) childhood meta-representational processing mechanism of false-belief development and those involved metacognitively in 'functional' delusions.

These psychological models of functioning all assert that difficulties faced by people in psychosis are the expression of some kind of abnormality in brain functioning. From a neuropsychological perspective, these abnormalities are hypothesized as being part of a 'connectivity' disorder. These connectivity differences have largely been found mainly in the frontal lobe of the brain, as well as in the connecting circuitry between the limbic and temporal lobes (Barch, 2005). This neuropsychological picture is an amalgamation of imaging studies, cognitive psychological experiments and electrophysiology. Neurocognitive impairments in psychosis describe a range of mild to severe difficulties with psychological skills (see Table 3.1, Penades and Catalan, 2012). This kind of research has led to the development of interventions that focus on the psychological skills impacted upon by the condition as opposed to the content or experience of the mental health issues itself.

Table 3.1 Severity of neurocognitive difficulties in schizophrenia (adapted from Penades and Catalan, 2012)

Mild difficulties	Moderate difficulties	Severe difficulties
Perceptual skills	Verbal memory	Executive function
Speed processing	Working memory	Verbal fluency
Recognition memory	Recall memory	Verbal learning
Naming	Visuo-motor skills	Motor speed
General intelligence	Distractability	Vigilance

Genetics and psychosis

Evidence for a genetic influence in psychosis is fairly compelling from behavioural genetic and molecular biological studies. A recent review of twin studies found that the variance attributable to the heritability of schizophrenia is about 84%; however, in all these kinds of studies, it is difficult to tease out the role of shared upbringing and learned psychological and social factors (Glatt et al., 2007). The genetic mechanisms through which this heritability is expressed remains largely unknown and presents a confused picture. There are many genes that are plausibly involved – i.e. there are candidate disease-related genes – but subsequent association analyses for these candidates have failed to establish 'empirical gene-wide' statistical significance (Tandon et al., 2008; Sanders et al., 2008).

Genetic epidemiological data is, however, beginning to produce a view that schizophrenia, bipolar affective disorder and other psychotic disorders such as schizoaffective disorder share some genetic liability (Owen et al., 2007). This presents another challenge to the empirical relevance to the categorical diagnostic distinctions made in the DSM-IV and ICD-10 manuals of diagnosis. The bottom line is that there is an increased risk by virtue of inheritability, for which the mechanisms remain unclear. This has led to a shift in favouring thinking that conditions such as autism, schizophrenia and attention-deficit-hyperactivity disorder (ADHD), rather than being unrelated diagnostic entities, instead represent a continuum of genetic and environmental neurodevelopmental impairment (Owen et al., 2011).

Call for autoethnographical accounts in nursing

Amongst mental health nurse theorists, there has been something of a persistent call for the development of increased ethnographic and auto-ethnographic accounts in mental health nursing research (Burnard, 2007; Foster et al., 2006; Grant, 2013). In some respects, this is fitting given the climate of recovery-oriented practice emerging in UK mental health practice (see Chapter 2). Critiques of how service-user experiences have been represented in professional literature (e.g. Grant, 2011) have noted how reductionist representations of individuals and their problems have gone unchallenged in professional literature. From a trans-modern perspective, this could be said to be legitimizing and socializing mental health professionals into a practice of 'othering'. Potential benefits for adopting such an approach include the development of reduced othering and power-related stigma, as well as the appreciation and implementation of the therapeutic power of self-narratives (Grant, 2011).

My own story, as partially presented here, seeks to illustrate with examples of lived experience the theoretical constructs espoused within the bio-psychiatric, meta-synthetic, neurocognitive, and various cognitive-psychological models. The profound shift in recognizing the role of abuse experiences and trauma in the aetiology of the psychoses is explored and reviewed. This places a demand upon mental health professionals, not just nursing, to make a significant skill shift in assessing the contribution of such experiences and in developing the availability of contextual third-wave therapeutic psychosocial (or nursing-social) skills in working with traumatic experiences (e.g. Dialectical Behavioural, Acceptance and Commitment, Mindfulness and values-based interventions). My autoethnographic account illustrates the emerging bio-psychiatric theory of aberrant salience and links this to supportive neuro-computational evidence. The current micro theories of cognitive psychology have been outlined and used to bridge into neurocognitive approaches to psychosis. Finally, a summary of genetic studies and how this has impacted the plausibility of diagnostic categorization of psychotic experiences was provided. The call for increased autoethnographic and ethnographically based qualitative research in mental health nursing and indeed in other professions was highlighted as a potential means of decreasing a social culture of legitimized othering in mental health clinical practice.

Chapter 4

A review of current UK treatment approaches to psychosis

Surveying contemporary interventions and their empirical status

A variety of current treatment approaches for psychosis are currently being researched and employed clinically. These are reviewed from a theoretical, evidence-based, implementational and autoethnographic perspective where relevant.

Metacognitive retraining approaches

Research into the socio-cognitive phenomenon of qualitatively different thinking styles and attributional biases has led to the development of a strand of so-called Metacognitive Therapeutic interventions. These reason that if problems with how we think about our thoughts (our metacognitive style) are significant to the onset of a psychosis, then helping the person to regain flexibility metacognitively ought to help with the subsequent unusual beliefs and thoughts. Early signs from a small controlled trial are that this kind of approach is well tolerated, non-harmful and leads to the self-report of subjective improvement and that, statistically – albeit non-significantly – the trend is towards a reduction in objective symptom scores (Aghotor et al., 2010). Larger-scale research with more participants is needed to more adequately evaluate the efficacy of such approaches. At present, preliminary trials are starting to indicate that this intervention is able to significantly improve on measures of theory of mind, social perception, emotional intelligence and social functioning (Rocha and Queiros, 2013) but show no differential benefits in terms of symptoms.

This kind of approach to working with psychosis is an example of a strong current trend of clinical psychological approach that seeks to improve a person's 'psychological flexibility' in response to experience, as opposed to the nature of the experience per se. Other examples of this include Dialectical Behavioural Therapy, Acceptance and Commitment

Therapy and Compassion-Focused Therapy, typically incorporating various kinds of Mindfulness-based approaches (Hayes, 2004; Kabat-Zinn, 1994; Chadwick et al., 2005; Gilbert, 2009). These constitute a raft of the so-called third wave of cognitive psychological therapies and more lately have become referred to as the 'contextual' approach (Grant et al., 2010).

Cognitive Remediation Therapy

Working on the basis of neuropsychological research in Cognitive Remediation Therapy, in a similar vein, Metacognitive Retraining aims to work with the psychological 'infrastructure' of the person's functioning rather than with the content or relationship to their experience. It seeks to improve the functioning of attention, memory, executive functions (e.g. decision making) and social cognition (i.e. thinking about other people's intentions) (Wykes et al., 2011). These kinds of treatment programmes include a range of cognitive skills tasks that are typically drilled and practiced: e.g. role-playing skills, problem-solving techniques, card-sorting tasks, interpreting and discussing social situations (Penades and Catalan, 2012). A meta-analysis of research undertaken so far by McGurk et al. (2007) indicates that Cognitive Remediation is associated with significant improvements across measures of 'cognitive performance', 'psychosocial functioning' and 'symptoms'. It's worth noting that the effect size of the improvement on symptoms was small and perhaps establishes that so-called cognitive impairment is to some degree relatively independent of other experiences of 'schizophrenia' (McGurk et al., 2007). It is possible that the symptom improvement is also indirect – that is the person experiences an improvement to self-esteem and self-efficacy (and thus mood) from the achievement of personal goals as a result of positive learning experiences from the intervention.

Mindfulness for psychosis interventions

Mindfulness, as a form of psychological intervention in the UK, is currently in its ascendency. It is currently incorporated into established contextual psychotherapies like Hayes's (2004) Acceptance and Commitment Therapy (ACT) and in Linehan's (1987) Dialectical Behavioural Therapy. Both of these therapeutic approaches can trace their roots into more 'classical' Cognitive-Behavioural Therapy, which has proven effective in the treatment of various kinds of anxiety difficulties and depression. They are both different in that they depart from the classical cognitive-behavioural approach by engaging more with the person's relationship to their experience rather than trying to help them wrestle directly with the content of the experience itself. A goal in these more contextualized accounts of our experience is to gain more flexibility in that experience rather than trying to 'correct' or 'alter' faulty patterns of thinking or perceptual inaccuracies.

The cognitive psychotherapies, it could be argued, constitute another branch of power-laden authority, this time within the professional domain largely of clinical psychology that could be said to be exerting a dominant narrative over the distressing experience of the service-user. Here, fault or blame for the experience is cast into the cognitions and perceptions of the individual and, in doing so, establishes the parameters of what is normal and acceptable, as well as what is not, and what constitutes a disorder or illness to be treated. Attempts to escape this organizationally and socially legitimized strand of technically authenticated oppression have advocated for others to attend to the meaning of the person's experience in its sociopolitical and cultural environment. In other words, what could be interpreted as a symptom of mental disorder – e.g. hearing a punishing controlling voice – could also be constructed and construed as a manifestation of pain and suffering. The former implies an underlying pathophysiological cause and legitimizes treatment and employing established orthodox professional responses. The latter seeks to comprehend the function of the distress and validate it.

Sociocultural learning and psychosis

A school of psychological thinking exemplified by the psychologist Vygotsky holds that our psychological experiences or phenomena are constructed from social activities. To put it another way, the "structures of higher mental functions represent a cast of collective social relations between people" (Vygotsky, 1998, p. 169). Culture consists of socially organized and mandated activities that include the development of agency (Ratner, 2000). The validity of this is apparent in the differentiation of the expression and cultural acceptability in the understanding of emotions across different cultures and indeed within cultures but transformed over time (see Keltner and Haidt, 1999).

In clinical psychology and psychiatry, the biological and neurophysiological influence of biological medicine places an emphasis on the physiological functioning and embodiment of emotional experiences. Yet our psychological development is also undeniably inextricably linked to our sociocultural experiential development. This much is evident in relation to psychosis from findings that negative emotions (e.g.

anxiety and depression) and respective negative beliefs about self and others in response to the experience of direct and indirect experiences of aggression (i.e. bullying) in childhood are mediators to the development of various kinds of paranoid thinking (e.g. ideas of social reference and persecution) (Melo et al., 2006).

Sociocultural influences on experience are also evident when clinical psychology classifies certain kinds of emotions as negative and others as positive inasmuch as our culture places value on avoiding or reducing negative experiences that are potential triggers. Not only do we tend not to culturally value (i.e. seek out or cherish) the so-called negative emotions (i.e. sadness, fear, anger, shame, guilt and so forth), we also place considerable stock in teaching and supporting one another to develop strategies to minimize the experience of such emotions and experiences. Such cultural norms and messages that we relay to one another serve to act as scaffolds for pathologizing certain kinds of experience. Contextually sensitive psychotherapeutic practices, such as those emerging from Mindfulness, seek to leverage a more value-free or value-positive reactivity to such experiences. Indeed, Romme and Escher (1993), in their work on people who hear voices, point out that those who do not have such a marked distress-laden relationship to their experience are able to function and thrive in their lives without the need for significant mental health service intervention.

Mindfulness for psychosis has largely entered into the treatment scene informed by the research work of Chadwick and colleagues (2005). It is a clinically promising intervention for people in reducing distress, and it is unsurprising that attempts to use and adapt this approach are beginning to happen with people with psychosis. Mindfulness is defined often in the literature as "paying attention in a particular way: on purpose, in the present moment and non-judgementally" (Kabat-Zinn, 1994, p. 4).

This definition has led to the proposal of a working model of Mindfulness (see Figure 4.1) that has had some early qualitative empirical

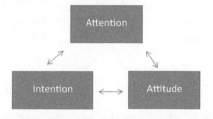

Figure 4.1 A proposed model of Mindfulness (reproduced with permission, from Shapiro et al., 2006)

validation (Shapiro et al., 2006). Kerr and colleagues (2012) undertook a sub-analysis of diaries completed by a group of participants involved in a randomized controlled trial exploring the efficacy of a kind of Mindfulness intervention called Mindfulness-Based Stress Reduction (MBSR). MBSR is a systematic approach to Mindfulness that also includes yoga exercises and has a proven track record of successfully reducing distress in a number of physical and psychological conditions. They found evidence of a qualitative shift in the descriptions of experiences provided by the participants in their reflective diary towards an emerging 'observing self' (Deikman, 1982), with attended increase in meta-awareness, reduction in self-identification, increased closeness and detail to the experience, less reactivity and increased non-judgemental observations. It's worth noting here that Kerr and colleagues (2012) found that in their sub-analysis one participant improved their Mindfulness scores and decreased their distress even though the initial experiences of Mindfulness were unpleasant. This bodes well for psychosis.

Chadwick and colleagues (2005) propose that a specific rationale for the use of Mindfulness is the intent on shifting towards a less judgemental and involved relationship to distressing intrusive experiences characterized medically as hallucinations and delusions. Their rationale is summarized in the Figure 4.2.

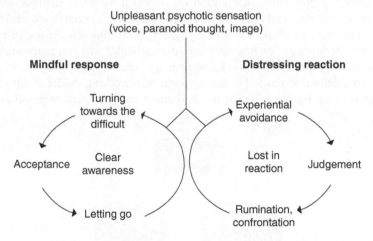

Figure 4.2 Rationale for Mindfulness for psychosis intervention (from Chadwick et al., 2005. © British Association for Behavioural and Cognitive Psychotherapies)

Chadwick and colleagues (2005, 2009) conducted an initial controlled trial that they have more recently replicated wherein people with a diagnosis of psychosis received Mindfulness as part of a group therapy programme and were compared to a waiting list group. This initial research was conducted due to a long-standing clinical caution in the use of meditation for people with psychosis and some sparse uncontrolled evidence of harmful effects from meditation practice (Yorston, 2001). The initial results showed a significant improvement in terms of general clinical functioning for those in the Mindfulness group, as well as significant increases in the ability to respond Mindfully to unpleasant experiences (Chadwick et al., 2005).

Acceptance and Commitment Therapy for psychosis

In contrast, several controlled trials of Acceptance and Commitment approaches have demonstrated effectiveness and also contain a considerable Mindfulness component (Bach and Hayes, 2002; Gaudiano and Herbert, 2006). Both of these studies found some evidence for the effectiveness of the intervention but, like the evidence and literature on Cognitive-Behavioural Therapy for psychosis, are subject to considerable critique and caution because of the lack of blinding in the conditions. This means effectively that there is the possibility of bias in the scoring of outcomes in the groups.

Acceptance and Commitment approaches to 'maladaptive behaviours' view them as unhealthy attempts to avoid or suppress thoughts, feelings or bodily sensations (Hayes, 2004). ACT works with clients to encourage them to abandon psychological strategies that seek to intentionally control experiences, alongside learning to accept the presence of difficult thoughts and feelings. This is combined with developing a focus on behaviours that produce individually valued outcomes and on how previous ways of coping with psychotic experiences may interfere with these. Through a combination of such approaches, the person is guided to learn how to notice without judgement the occurrence of unwanted private experiences without engaging in a power struggle with them.

Metacognitive Therapy for psychosis

Metacognitive Therapy (MCT) (Wells, 2009) is an approach that assumes that emotional distress (the presence of pain associated with emotional experiences) is related to unhelpful processes like worry, rumination, threat focus and attempts to control thoughts. These kinds of psychological processes are hypothesized to be linked to beliefs about thoughts (or metacognitive beliefs) that fall into the domains of usefulness, controllability and the dangerousness of such experiences. So, for example having a belief about worry that it is 'uncontrollable' will result in the continuation or maintenance of emotional distress because the person feels helpless in the face of their emotional experience (Fisher and Wells, 2005, 2008). MCT encourages the person to develop a more detached awareness of their thoughts and to work on unhelpful attentional strategies rather than evaluate the validity and usefulness of their thoughts themselves (à la Cognitive-Behavioural Therapy, CBT) (Wells, 2009).

An early exploratory trial of MCT for psychosis has established that this approach is well tolerated (as evidenced by a low rate of attrition, or dropout, in the participation of people in the trial) and that it leads to clinically significant reductions in measures of psychiatric symptoms (using the PANSS symptom scales) (Hutton et al., 2014). As is acknowledged in the research, this is a non-randomized, non-blinded trial, and therefore it is highly likely that the observed and recorded improvements are subject to bias on the part of the assessor. As such, an RCT (randomized controlled trial) is needed to establish the efficacy of the intervention.

Cognitive-Behavioural Therapy (CBT) for psychosis

CBT for psychosis is the most well developed and researched psychological intervention. Whilst CBT remains a recommended form of intervention by NICE (National Institute of Health Care Excellence, 2009), there remains significant controversy over its efficacy. Jones and colleagues' (2012) recent systematic review showed no significant difference between CBT over other kinds of psychotherapeutic interventions in reducing the risk of relapse. Zimmerman and colleagues (2005) found, in their meta-analysis of randomized control trials, that it has 'moderate effectiveness' in the reduction of symptoms, although this has been strongly challenged in Lynch and fellows' (2010) meta-analysis that addressed methodological shortcomings and concluded that once these had been controlled for there is no 'statistically significant effect'.

Whilst there are a significant number of published meta-analyses of CBT's efficacy in symptom reduction in psychosis (wherein it may be germaine at this point to raise question marks about equating psychological therapy with pharmacological therapy), few of these have rigorously looked at the effect of blindedness on the study effect sizes. Unpopular as it may be within clinical psychological circles, there is a clear distorting 'magnification' effect. Poorly controlled studies lead to the development of a body of evidence that over-inflate outcomes and muddy the efficacy of interventions with sources of bias. Amalgamate these studies and undertake meta-analysis without due care and attention to the sources of those biases, and there is the risk of perseveration of the inflation of efficacy.

Lynch and colleagues' (2010) meta-analysis has not been without critique. Kingdon (2010) identifies that the inclusion criteria and study selection approach used in the meta-analysis would lead to the exclusion of some study trials that report moderately large effect sizes in favour of CBT. These include studies in which the comparison arm consists of treatment as usual conditions and studies in which hospitalization is used as a measure of relapse. It is also worth noting that this landmark meta-analysis focuses on end-of-treatment outcome scoring. This leads to the exclusion of data from trials that look at effect changes at longer periods of follow-up.

There is no doubt that the practice of conducting RCTs as a research methodology for teasing out the efficacy and effectiveness of psychological therapies is itself a contested process (Stirman et al., 2005). Collections of such evidence and the approaches best used to collect robust meta-analytical data are similarly beset with methodological difficulties (Lynch et al., 2010). So far, meta-analyses prior to the trend-bucking paper by Lynch and colleagues (2010) have concluded that CBT has a small to moderate effect size with respect to symptom reduction for psychosis. Whom are we to believe, especially in light of the counter-critique raised by Kingdon (2010)? Research into the use of psychological therapy for psychosis continues undaunted, and publications discussing the effectiveness of CBT for psychosis include Lynch and fellows' (2010) review with caveats (Sivec and Montesano, 2012). It seems that the evidence base for CBT as the dominant form of psychological intervention has been roundly shaken. As yet, it remains dominant and arguably chronically underutilized for all that (Kingdon and Kirschen, 2006).

It is worth considering here what is being contested. Effect sizes are the standardized mean differences between two groups. Using terms like 'small', 'medium' and 'large' out of context is a dangerous practice. The effectiveness of one particular intervention can really be interpreted only in relation to other interventions that are intent on producing the same effect (Glass et al., 1981). Clinical interventions are almost always evaluated in terms of their potential health–economic benefit. It is also possible that small, expensive changes induced by treatment could still be very individually significant if this effect were cumulative or maintained over time and, say, made the difference between unbearable suffering and a tolerable experience. This kind of research, however, shows mean changes in scores in large groups and makes the argument for the efficacy of an intervention in a broad and non-specific way. It does not provide the kind of individualized specific information about the experience of the intervention that is often of more use to the person and mental health professional alike.

The clinical experience of delivering CBT for psychosis

CBT for psychosis is a carefully tailored treatment approach that is highly individualized for the person rather than a 'package intervention'. As such, there are relatively few manualized approaches, and those that do exist tend to advocate the need for individualized formulation with the client (Fowler et al., 1995). The role of emotion in psychosis has come under increased scrutiny in empirical research and either is proposed to constitute a central role in the development of symptoms (Freeman and Garety, 2003) or can be considered an underlying contribution to the development of persecutory experiences by others (e.g. Bentall et al., 1994). As such, amongst academics, there is no consensus over the mechanisms and role of emotional experiences in psychosis, although there is no doubt that those who experience psychosis are significantly emotionally affected particularly in terms of trauma, low self-esteem and depression (Barrowclough et al., 2003).

CBT treatments for psychosis have in common a goal of targeting the distress associated with the experience of unusual thoughts, beliefs and perceptions (Fowler et al., 1995). Typically, a stress-vulnerability model is slowly introduced to the person as a rationale for working psychologically (Zubin and Spring, 1977). This rationale is essentially that an individual's vulnerability to unusual experiences is an interaction of their experience of distressing life events coupled with either inborn or acquired insufficient coping mechanisms or styles that contribute to the experience of psychosis.

Formulations focus on the experience of specific 'symptoms' wherein the person experiences emotional distress. It leads to focusing on understanding and modifying the factors that exacerbate distress and behavioural disturbance. In order to reach this point, there is a considerable emphasis and commonality within CBT for psychosis treatment approaches on engagement with the person. Initially, the opportunity to talk at length about concerns and to develop a rapport and trust is held as key. Paying particular attention to the therapeutic relationship and issues around collaboration is emphasized.

Table 4.1 An A-B-C Formulation Approach, or cross-sectional case formulation in CBT

A: Antecedent (or precipitant)	B: Belief (about self/ others/the world)	C: Consequence
'I went out downtown to go shopping and feeling odd. I saw someone looking at me intently as I walked into the shop'.	'They thought there was something wrong with me'. 'They were thinking this because they could hear what I was thinking'.	'Feel highly anxious and intruded upon. Left the shop rapidly without buying anything and returned home. Felt miserable'.

In the Freeman and colleagues (2002) approach to extreme false beliefs (or delusions), a cross-sectional approach to understanding the person's distress is used. A common model for this is the A-B-C formulation shown in Table 4.1.

This kind of formulation can then leverage a number of different pieces of research on cognitive biases in psychosis, as addressed in Chapter 3. Here, there is the possibility that the person is 'jumping to conclusions' and is also engaging in 'mind reading'. They are also clearly externally attributing their experience. Capturing as much detail as possible about the antecedent events can often help generate evidence of this. Here are some pertinent questions to ask. Were there other people in the shop (and did you notice whether they also were looking at you)? How did you appear – what were you wearing or doing or saying when you went into the shop (i.e. were you wearing or doing anything that might have caught their attention)? This kind of guided discovery – done gently and from the perspective of genuine curiosity on the part of the therapist – can facilitate dialogue that seeks to identify potential thinking errors and also generate alternative more evidence-based explanations for other behaviours that are less personalized than those currently being employed. These can sometimes be developed into specific behavioural experiments to test such assumptions and beliefs that can in turn reduce paranoia and social anxiety.

An example in using CBT behavioural experiments

As an example from my clinical experience in working with someone with such paranoia, one ongoing strategy they had developed was to dress in a fashion that they hoped reduced attention to themselves and made themselves feel 'safer' (e.g. dark sunglasses, hat, hooded jackets etc.).

This safety behaviour made them feel, in the short term, more secure about being out but also had the undesired effect of making them more noticeable to others. We challenged this together through a relatively non-threatening observational experiment. We agreed to undertake it in a local café, and the client was positioned in the shop in advance with a coffee. As therapist, I entered the café dressed in the manner that the client preferred and acting in a way to minimize the amount of interaction I had with others. The client was asked to pay particular attention to how many people stopped to look at me and how long they paid attention to me. In a subsequent visit a while later, the client paid attention to others when I entered the shop without these safety behaviours in action. This led to a discussion about what they had observed and what sense they made of other people's behaviours and reactions to me when I presented myself to them in these different ways.

Freeman and colleagues' (2002) approach to formulation involves co-understanding a 'search for meaning' in response to experiences that are usually ambiguous but perceived as significant. It thus in some respects synthesizes aspects of established cognitive bias research, Frith's theory of mind model where there can be problems in reading the intentions of others and the underpinning theory of aberrant salience (Kapur, 2003; Chapter 3 of this volume).

Increasingly, in addition to using more 'classical' CBT approaches to these unusual thoughts, cognitive approaches to psychosis will incorporate aspects of Mindfulness. This is evident in Freeman and colleagues' (2006) self-help text on overcoming paranoid interpretations. It advocates the person practices becoming a 'detached observer of their fears' (i.e. using Mindfulness of emotions and thoughts), tests out suspicious thoughts actively rather than just accepting them, learns to 'let go' of suspicious thoughts if they come (developing the non-stick, or Teflon, mind) and reduces time spent worrying about paranoid thoughts.

In working with people to adopt these approaches, the therapist needs to engage in a number of different practices. It is important to adopt a 'voyage of discovery' attitude (Kingdon and Turkington, 2005), which is another way of expressing the long-standing, so-called CBT Colombo approach (Grant et al., 2010). This is a reference to the enquiring attitude adopted by the TV detective who strives to understand what has happened in the investigation. The therapist is genuinely interested in understanding what leads to the unusual belief. This is vital because the false belief is typically held together by evidence powerful enough to support and maintain it (Maher, 1974). Understanding what this evidence is and how other forms of discomfirmatory evidence are being overlooked or actively excluded is helpful in putting together alternative approaches and behavioural experiments to challenge and ultimately weaken the conviction in such beliefs. Bear in mind, from the thinking-style research covered in Chapter 3, that people with paranoia often require less evidence to sustain the conviction in their beliefs. At the same time, being genuinely empathetic with the emotional distress these beliefs can provoke in the person is vital. It is important not simply to collude with the account but not at the cost of failing to empathize with how distressing the experience must be. So, typical responses that validate the person's emotional reactions whilst leaving the therapist free to re-examine the evidence supporting the beliefs and help the person look for alternative interpretations are for example, 'This must be really anxiety provoking for you' and 'Worrying that the neighbours are out to harm you must be a really distressing thing to deal with'.

Relatively few detailed qualitative analyses explore the experience of Cognitive-Behavioural Therapy for psychosis, and this is an area that desperately requires further research so that the given techniques and approaches can be better understood in terms of how they impact. CBT therapists are at pains to be sensitive to the impact of dialogue in the moment, but systematic research of a qualitative nature can uncover valuable guidance on the do's and don'ts of particular therapeutic approaches. In one of the few studies published, Messari and Hallam (2003) undertook a discourse analysis of people's experience of CBT for psychosis. It makes for informative reading even with the very small number of participants. For some, the experience of guided discovery was liberating and enabled them to make sense of their beliefs and come to an understanding of them. This was aided by the existence of a 'friendship discourse' – that is where therapy is construed as a meeting of two equals and thereby of experiencing therapy as a 'collaborative enterprise'. Interestingly, for one participant where the therapist had been reluctant and had not openly discussed the purpose and goals of therapy, there was a parallel sense of powerlessness. Padesky (1993) has long argued (and continues to do so; see Padesky et al., 2011) for the need for therapists to be guided by genuine curiousity and to view Socratic questioning as a form of guided discovery, rather than a process of leading the person to change their mind about things.

Antipsychotic medication for psychosis

The mainstay of treatment for psychosis in the UK remains the use of 'antipsychotic' medications. I've placed the scare-quotes around the word because those critical of medication approaches call into question the validity of being so specific about the action of these medicines (Moncrieff, 2009). Antipsychotics are psychotropic agents that currently fall into the categories of either second-generation antipsychotic (SGA), or atypicals, or first-generation antipsychotic, or typicals. These categorizations refer to the difference between older and newer kinds of antipsychotic drugs. SGAs (for example olanzapine, quetiapine, risperidone and clozapine) have a lower affinity and occupancy for dopaminergic receptors and additional occupancy for serotoninergic receptors, as well as some others. These drugs have a somewhat different neurochemical action to their predecessors and are typically believed to have a lowered rate of side effect because of this (Lieberman et al., 2008). There is some doubt about this claim, however, as it may simply be more of a reflection of more judiciously cautious lower dosage of the SGA antipsychotic in comparison to the older medicines (Leucht et al., 2009).

Leucht colleagues' (2009) recent meta-analysis of placebo-controlled trials evaluated the pooled effectiveness of SGAs on measures of overall symptoms and found that, overall, the effect was one of a 'small' to 'moderate' effect size. Bearing in mind the caveats established earlier on effect sizes, it's worth noting a critical point. This combined effect size does not take into account a notable so-called file-drawer problem (Iyengar and Greenhouse, 1988). This is where there is a publication bias (Rosenthal, 1979) and studies that have produced a non-significant result or negative result have been suppressed.

This is problematic for meta-analysis because it is important to collect all rigourous studies – published or otherwise – if the subsequent conclusions are to be valid. Including studies where there is a non-representative proportion of studies giving results in a positive direction will lead to an overestimation biased towards positivity. This is indeed a parallel point of contention we have explored regarding the current state of analysis of the CBT evidence: have sufficient rigorous studies been conducted that demonstrate effects one way or the other with respect to the null hypothesis and that enable us to confidently form the appropriate scientific conclusions (Kingdon, 2010)?

Interestingly Leucht and colleagues (2009) conducted the initial funnel plot of standard error on their data, demonstrating a pronounced and statistically significant asymmetry. They do not go on to apply the corrective computational algorithm on their pooled effect sizes to estimate the impact of missing studies on the meta-analysis (Duval and Tweedie, 2000). In some bio-statistical simulations of the scale of effect size changes that occur as a result of publication bias, it's clear that the direction of inferences can be influenced (Duval and Tweedie, 2000). It is possible therefore that, for some bodies of research, the nature of the inference can be changed if all studies of the phenomenon can be made available for evaluation and inclusion. More conservatively, it is likely that the effect sizes of antipsychotic efficacy are being overestimated in this study simply by virtue of publication bias alone, let alone other potential sources of bias (e.g. author allegiance), even in the most rigorously conducted study.

Leucht colleagues' (2009) analysis reviewed 150 double-blind RCTs that compared second-generation, or atypical, antipsychotic drugs for overall efficacy on positive and negative symptoms of psychosis versus first-generation drugs. Only four second-generation medications were found to be better than first-generation medication for overall efficacy with small to medium effect sizes: amisulpiride, clozapine, olanzapine and risperidone (95% confidence interval, -0.31 $p = 0.0001$, -0.52 $p = 0.0001$, -0.28 $p = 0.0001$ and -0.13 $p = 0.002$). Indeed, there has been a strong critique of the use of antipsychotic medication that the efficacy of the treatments have been over-stated because of methodological flaws in the research procedures (i.e. blinding and masking biases and publication biases) (Morrison et al., 2012). It is interesting to see that research into the efficacy of drug treatments is labouring under the same academic critical attacks as that of research into the efficacy of CBT.

Leucht and colleagues (2009) critique the idea of these relatively heterogeneous medications being grouped as a class of atypical drugs. They point out that they do not consistently have an effect on so-called negative symptoms that has been used clinically as a justification for the title 'atypical'. They also do not have a consistent or common side-effect profile that has been another justification for the use of 'atypical'. There is some evidence that, for second-generation antipsychotic medications, the dissociation time is considerably shorter than for first-generation medications (Seeman, 2002). This means that for certain neuro-receptors – specifically the D2 sub-receptor type of the neurochemical dopamine – the amount of time that the medication 'blocks' these receptors is relatively short. This is also known as the 'fast-off-D2' theory (Seeman, 2002). In spite of this, large trials of the tolerability of second-generation vs. first-generation medications have not borne out the hoped-for advantage in a reduced side-effect profile (Peluso et al., 2012). Indeed, one of the issues in research trials that established second-generation side-effect profiles was the use of haloperidol as the comparator drug, a first-generation medication with relatively high extra-pyramidal syndrome (EPS) liability (Peluso et al., 2012). EPS side effects are particularly difficult to tolerate as a result of activation of the brain's extra-pyramidal system that coordinates and controls movement. Hence EPS effects include akasthisia, or a state of agitated restlessness, muscle spasms and contractions, shakiness and gait problems.

Moncrieff (2009) is a strong critic amongst psychiatrists of the use of medication as the mainstay of treatment approaches to psychosis and other conditions. She critiques the idea that antipsychotics are just that – i.e. antipsychotic – and they lead to a 'dulling' of all thoughts and an indifference (Moncrieff, 2009). She has further suggested that longer-term use of antipsychotic medication may exacerbate the likelihood of subsequent psychotic episodes. One proposed potential mechanism for this is via pharmacodynamic stress; that is the sustained blockade of neurochemical receptors results in a brain adaptation response (so-called dopamine supersensitivity) (Viguera et al., 1997). If the person abruptly withdraws their medication, then the treatment no longer acts in opposition to the brain's neuro-adaptation, and this might explain the recurrence of psychotic episodes. This is an alternative to the it's-a-relapse-of-their-illness/disease-process argument that has been used as an indirect form of support for the use of antipsychotic medications. The so-called dopamine hypothesis, after all, rather depends on the suppression of symptoms as a result of antipsychotic use.

This theory seems to be borne out by the longer-term observational study of Harrow and Jobe (2013) that looked at the recovery rates of people with psychosis who abstain from long-term antipsychotic therapy. Whilst there is little controversy over the efficacy of antipsychotics to have useful effects on symptoms in the short term, they are not universally effective inasmuch as even those fully compliant with such treatment may continue to experience symptoms of psychosis and indeed a 'relapse' of the condition (Haddock and Lewis, 1996).

Harrow and Jobe's (2013) longitudinal study followed people with a diagnosis of schizophrenia of various types and followed them over time to track their experience of psychotic symptoms, hospital admissions and use of antipsychotic medication. As such, it has been able to compare the long-term efficacy of antipsychotic treatment as it also followed participants who remained medication free. The data from their 20-year study indicate that a high percentage of those prescribed antipsychotics continued to experience 'psychotic activity' at most (4–5/6) of the follow-up years. A significant minority of those without prolonged antipsychotic use showed more favourable outcomes (Harrow and Jobe, 2013). This study is not on its own in suggesting that beyond two or three years, the effectiveness of antipsychotic medications may significantly change.

Wunderink and colleagues (2013) undertook an RCT that compared rates of recovery following first-episode psychosis after a seven-year follow-up when randomly assigned to either a maintenance treatment arm or a reduction/discontinuation arm of the trial. In their study, patients in the reduction/discontinuation arm experienced twice the recovery rate of the maintenance treatment arm (40.7% vs. 17.6%).

A common concern and source of contention is the potential neuro-toxicity of antipsychotic medication (and indeed the converse potential neuroprotective benefit) (Moncrieff, 2009). It remains controversial and equivocal as to whether long-term structural and functional brain changes that happen in the progression of psychosis are being amelio-rated or amplified by the respective medication treatments (Smieskova et al., 2009). It is clear that there are longitudinal changes in the brains of people with psychosis over time, most notably grey-matter volume reduction and enlargement of the ventricles, and the potential confound-ing effect of antipsychotic treatment remains debatable (Smieskova et al., 2009; Job et al., 2005). It is possible that antipsychotic treatment attenuates these longer-term structural brain changes and requires imag-ing research to conduct studies on people with psychosis who are medi-cation free. Given recent developments in longitudinal research into the recovery of people without medication use, along with some advances in the adoption and suitability of psychological treatments for those who abstain from using medicines, the prospect of undertaking such research no longer seems quite as remote as it did only a decade or so ago.

There is a growing consensus that the efficacy of antipsychotic medications has been overstated through artifacts and bias in research evidence, but, nonetheless, certainly in the short-term (as in the first 2–3 years of experiencing psychosis), these medicines have a significant role to play in reducing distress and the experience of symptoms. Despite this, there is a considerable risk to using such medications, and studies of time to discontinuation (e.g. Lieberman et al., 2008) show that there is relatively little to choose from between new forms of medication in this regard. Full compliance with medication is no guarantee of full 'control' of the experiences of psychosis, and indeed, from emerging evidence of the longer-term use of antipsychotic medications for some people with psychosis, there is a positive advantage to gently withdrawing and discontinuing from their usage with suitable professional support (Har-row and Jobe, 2013; Wunderink et al., 2013). There remains a need for developing viable psychological and psychosocial approaches to work-ing with psychosis precisely because of the considerable disadvantage of longer-term medication-based treatments (Chadwick, 2005).

Cognitive-Behavioural Therapy for psychosis has come under considerable critique in terms of the viability of its research evidence (Lynch et al., 2010). These critiques are, in of themselves, not unimpeachable, and there are long-standing questions of the validity of positivistic scientific approaches to this kind of social science phenomena. The utility of quantitative research findings to the dilemmas that confront clinical health and social care workers remains a contestable point. The need for continued qualitative research into the experience of therapy approaches – good *and* bad – remains as vital if not more so than rigorous RCTs. New forms of contextualized psychological therapy and therapies based on neuropsychological understandings of psychosis remain in need of concerted research and clinical appraisal. It is also worthwhile mentioning that there are developing approaches to working with psychosis that I haven't covered here either because they are not sufficiently well researched or prevalent in the UK (e.g. Open Dialogue approaches) or because they will be covered in the subsequent chapter on recovery-focused approaches – e.g. the recovery college approach (see Chapter 5).

THE LIVED EXPERIENCE OF USING ANTIPSYCHOTIC MEDICATION TREATMENT

My own experience of treatment is limited largely to using a variety of medications and two inpatient stays, one voluntary and one under section 2 of the Mental Health Act. I was treated using a variety of what are now considered to be the older, or typical, kinds of antipsychotic medication – namely stellazine, haloperidol and chlorpromazine. I also experienced the use of the depot preparation modecate, or fluphenazine decanoate. (A depot is a long-acting antipsychotic medication delivered by deep-muscular injection.)

The experience of unwanted effects

Each of these medications produced difficult side effects for me. A common feature (regardless of the medication) was that of feeling 'dampened' and that I was thinking through porridge. This is not commonly referred to in the scientific literature on

antipsychotic medication. It was a feeling of persistent 'fuzziness' and difficult to articulate. I can liken it to the experience
of being hung-over without the pleasurable use of alcohol the
night before. Thoughts seemed difficult and slow to produce,
and I also found at times that the quality of my speaking voice
seemed impaired – sort of muted and without its regular tonal
range. It is possible this was a mild form of laryngeal dystonia,
although it never received any specific medical attention. It was a
difference that I noticed and caused me some frustration and distress. It reinforced for me my 'otherness'. It was a considerable
relief to recover from these difficulties when I eventually stopped
the use of antipsychotic treatment.

The most distressing unwanted effect from the medication was
a period of sustained and severe muscle-locking, or dystonia. This
was focused largely around my neck and shoulders, although
I also experienced it in my legs and arms. This was excruciatingly
painful and was relieved only by drug-induced sleep and waiting
out the half-life of the medication. I struggled at times with some
disturbances to my gait (a tendency for my legs to 'over-swing'
and lock out whilst walking) and with severe agitation, or akasthisia. This was a particularly distressing experience – the urge to
pace, with restless legs and an inability to bear being seated or
still at times. This sensation, when it was present, never seemed
to dull in intensity or go away at any point until finally resolved.
I recall being treated with some procyclidine, which was a particularly bitter-tasting medication if you didn't swallow it completely
at once.

I can recall having CAT (computer axial tomography) brain
scans to examine the functioning of my brain. These came back
'clear' – whatever that meant – and then peculiarly the inpatient
staff treating me seemed to berate me when they found me struggling with some aspect of restlessness or my gait. It was as if there
was no reason in their eyes for there to be any difficulties neu-
rologically because of the all-clear scan, and they seemed to be
acting on the assumption that I was intentionally manifesting these
experiences. This was, as you might expect, a very demeaning

experience and one that created a great deal of tension with the staff. I can only surmise in retrospect that a lack of understanding and knowledge about the neurological unwanted effects of the medication led the staff to act in this way.

Thankfully for me, I seemed to develop a tolerance to these aspects of the medication in time, and the experiences of these unwanted effects largely wore off. With the exception of the mental fuzziness – an impairment to the qualitative experience of mental flow – these unwanted effects subsided. They were then later replaced with some motor tics (i.e. 'pill-rolling' – which is then unconscious rubbing of the finger and thumb tips as though the person is rolling a pill in their fingers) and the dreaded weight gain. I also found I had at times something of a 'shiny skin', or excess greasiness. This was particularly noticeable to me around my forehead. Naturally, none of these experiences did anything positive for my self-image or self-esteem and tended to reinforce experiences of paranoia ("People are looking at me for some reason") as I did tend to stick out!

Therapeutic effects

I find it very difficult to be clear about what the more desirable effects of the medication was. Even after several weeks and indeed months of being on the regular doses, I still found myself experiencing, at times, unusual thoughts that had no obvious factual basis (delusions) and particularly ideas of reference. These were the most persistent experiences of psychosis that I had. Occasionally, there were times when I had visual experiences and saw things that others weren't experiencing. At my most generous, I might say that the medication reduced how often I had these experiences, but it is obviously very difficult to say. There was a point, however, where I was not troubled by any of these kinds of experiences and was largely struggling more with my mood, confidence and self-worth in particular. By this time, I was being treated by depot injection, presumably because staff seemed to doubt whether I was continuously taking my medication as prescribed. Perhaps the occasional 'breakthroughs' in obvious disturbed perception led them to question whether I was consistently taking the medication. I was taking it – it simply didn't help to resolve all of these strange experiences.

Once discharged into community care and no longer under the constant scrutiny of staff members, I continued to be entirely compliant with medication. I took, along with the depot injection, antidepressant medication, the side-effect medicine, and a mood stabilizer that was, if memory serves, a hefty dose of carbamazepine.

It was difficult to think through all this stuff. I'd been on a variety of antidepressants and, having been on venlafaxine for at least six months with no discernable improvement subjectively to my mood and emotional well-being, I protested to the GP that I'd like a break from taking these tablets. Fortunately for me, he agreed with me, and I was able to wean myself off the antidepressant and cut it down fairly rapidly over the course of a couple of weeks. I did the same with the mood stabilizer and noticed that I was less 'foggy' and starting to feel more alert. This had, I suppose, a tiny knock-on effect on my overall well-being because at least I felt that I was a little more in touch with myself and my faculties and that I'd been able to take some kind of control of the treatment regime. All of this came from me, however; it wasn't on the agenda of my care coordinator to discuss coming off treatment at any stage. I refused my depot one day, politely but firmly, and that was the last time I saw my community psychiatric nurse!

At this point, I was living in sheltered accommodation that had 24-hour staffing. I suppose that the team, given I was living where I was with staff oversight, considered me less of a risk. Were I to fall unwell again (as they seemed keen to prophesy during my sparse consultations with the locum psychiatrist of the moment), I guess they thought that staff would pick up on this and they could swing into action with more appointments or a Mental Health Act assessment. Naturally, this is a somewhat gloomy and pessimistic state of affairs to be living under and didn't really do much for my overall mood. It thus wasn't until I managed to move out from the sheltered accommodation into private housing and then subsequently sack my community team's involvement that I was able to make significant improvements to my daily living. I found that going into hiding from services and then reinventing myself to get a new job were amongst the biggest things that contributed to recovering from the acute phases of psychosis.

Chapter 5

Research into recovery from psychosis

An empirical review and critical reflection

This chapter seeks to review the current state of evidence on the development of recovery-focused approaches to psychosis. It will outline contemporary critical conceptual and research methodological issues. It will adopt a lens of post-structural and post-modern critique and also speak to the rise of lived experience of recovery.

The state of recovery research

It is worth reflecting here that I think this is one of the relatively few occasions where research is perhaps somewhat in advance of clinical practice. There is now in the UK a development commitment from government-driven and professional-driven agendas to implement recovery that is influencing the construction and delivery of services (e.g. Royal College of Psychiatrists and Care Services Improvement Partnership, 2007; Department of Health, 2006). This does not preclude there being the dreaded research–practice gap that academic nursing professionals, amongst others, have profited from writing about exhaustively in the past four decades. My contention here also inevitably foreshadows the politics of recovery, which I cover in considerable depth in Chapter 7. Wherever there are statutory organizations staffed by human beings, inevitably there will be personal and also professional political agendas that obfuscate the delivery of empirically validated care (Rycroft-Malone, 2006). Given that recovery also espouses the need for organizational change, there will be inevitable inequities in the fidelity of systems of recovery-focused care implemented in health and social care organizations with long-standing treatment-focused models of care (Slade et al., 2014). As Perkins and Slade (2012) put it, "a disjunction remains between policy and practice, with organizational policies espousing a recovery orientation and teams re-branding as 'recovery and support' teams, whilst pursuing clinical practices which prioritize symptomatic treatment rather than recovery support" (p. 29).

In a trans-modernist sense, the development of recovery-oriented practice could be partially viewed as an institutional–organizational reaction to the persistent, growing, collective voices of 'interpellation' present in service-user survivor accounts (Dussel, 1995). Research academics have to some degree acted as a conduit for this voice via qualitative research and the endorsement of lived experience as a legitimate form of truth and knowledge. Academia and research have also formed a medium for the 'translation' of user-originated appeals to the authority of health care providers (psychiatry, the NHS and its incumbent professional groups therein) to enact change to injustices experienced by those within and about the system of mental health care. This can be seen by the bringing to bear of empirical frameworks and approaches (of high cultural validity to the evidence-based practitioners of mental health care) to the lived experience of recovery. This organizational translational process has also, I would argue, been accelerated by the increased representation of recovered persons within academic and professional spheres of the orthodoxy. The creation of 'desirable' employee personal characteristics, like the experience of mental health difficulties and also positive discrimination in the recruitment of new professionals, has to some extent served to legitimize this kind of knowledge (Tait and Lester, 2005).

Leamy and colleagues (2011) for example have published the first systematic review and narrative synthesis of 'personal recovery' by reviewing 97 published studies recounting a conceptualization of personal recovery. Their synthesis identified five categorical themes of recovery processes – as summarized in Table 5.1, and this constitutes a main part of a conceptual framework for recovery.

Andresen and colleagues (2003) have also identified from recovery narratives a stage model of recovery. People recovering from psychosis undergo a five-stage process of Moratorium, Awareness, Preparation, Rebuilding and Growth. We therefore now have a well-established, scientific evidence base developed from personal recovery stories of those in recovery and an understanding of the critical ingredients for recovery processes and the stages of recovery that people typically progress through. This kind of knowledge base is being developed out of the collective synthesis and analysis of lived experiences of those who have made a successful personal recovery and demonstrates the utility of mixed-method approaches.

Table 5.1 CHIME framework (adapted from Leamy et al., 2011, p. 448)

Connectedness	Hope and optimism about the future	Identity	Meaning in life	Empowerment
Peer support	Belief in the possibility of recovery	Dimensions of identity	Meaning of mental illness experiences	Personal responsibility
Relationships	Motivation to change	Rebuilding/ redefining positive sense of identity	Spirituality	Control over life
Support from others	Hope-inspiring relationships	Overcoming stigma	Quality of life	Focusing on strengths
Being part of the community	Positive thinking and valuing success		Meaningful life and social roles	
	Having dreams and aspirations		Meaningful life and social goals Rebuilding life	

Strategies to cope with life stress and experiences of psychosis

Phillips and colleagues (2009) conducted a systematic review of qualitative and quantitative research studies into the strategies of people living with the experience of psychosis. Lived experience forms a potentially useful source of expertise for professionals and people experiencing psychosis. (See Table 5.2.)

Le Boutillier and colleagues (2011) conducted a systematic review of qualitative literature that offer recovery-oriented practice guidance. This led to the construction of an interpretative analysis of the key ingredients of recovery-oriented practice as currently conceptualized in the international professional literature. The superordinate domains of these were promoting citizenship, organizational commitment, supporting personally defined recovery and working relationships. These domains

Table 5.2 Coping strategies used by people experiencing psychosis (adapted from Phillips et al., 2009)

Strategies used to cope with psychotic experiences and distress		
Ignore experiences/ ignoring voices	Self-instruction/self-talk	Avoiding conflict
Selective listening to voices/setting limits on their influences	Decrease activity/ minimize external stimuli	Avoiding overexertion
Competing auditory stimulation (yelling or talking back), humming, watching TV, listening to music, repeating numbers subvocally	Increase activity/ distraction	Taking regular medication
Sleeping	Reduce arousal	Adhering to a regulated lifestyle
Prayer	Self-stimulation	Engaging in work or leisure
Meditation	Social relations	Withdrawal
Focus on one thing at a time	Inward attention	Increased interpersonal contact
Sports/exercise	Adaptive learning	Proper diet/self-care

provide new professional foci within mental health work. For example within the domain of promoting citizenship, there is the suggestion that twenty-first-century mental health professionals must necessarily engage with the need to become social activists to challenge stigma and to support people recovering from psychosis in accessing community resources, within which citizenship flourishes, and overcoming barriers to doing so.

This might include for example the mental health professional seeking to break down barriers in accessing employment and proactively engaging in challenging discrimination within workplaces. It also suggests that professional mental health work involves lobbying local and centralized government on issues that obstruct citizenship. Take for example the recent furore over the government's assessment system for benefits and fitness for work as being grossly inappropriate for people with mental health difficulties (Weatherhead et al., 2014). This has led to diverse groups of mental health professionals, amongst other concerned citizens collaborating via social media forums such as Twitter,

Table 5.3 Summary of REFOCUS trial recovery-focused interventions (adapted from Slade et al., 2011)

Recovery-focused (REFOCUS) interventions
Understanding values and treatment preferences
Supporting goal striving
Strengths assessment
Working with staff values and knowledge related to recovery
Coaching skills and partnership working

providing evidence for the proposed reform of sociopolitical policies and procedures (see for example Weatherhead et al., 2014). Such kinds of intervention and activities are not traditionally seen as a legitimate nursing activity within the treatment-focused mental health organization. Implementing recovery-focused work is thus contributing to broadening the developing milieu of nursing and mental health professional activity.

Building on the fundamental empirical research on recovery for psychosis already undertaken, the Slade and colleagues' (2011) research group is currently undertaking a large-cluster RCT (randomized controlled trial) to evaluate the efficacy of recovery-focused interventions called the REFOCUS trial. Using the conceptual framework outlined by Leamy and fellows' (2011) systematic review and narrative synthesis of the literature on recovery and established measures of recovery, they are evaluating the impact of attempts to foster recovery-focused practice in secondary mental health care services in the UK. The interventions outlined in their REFOCUS manual (Bird et al., 2011) outlines the model of working practice shown in Table 5.3.

Supporting goal striving within a personal recovery vision and values base

These elements of practice already have supporting evidence independently of each other. Clarke and colleagues (2009) outline the theory and practice of collaborative goal striving within the context of collaborative goal setting. Goal setting is already widely recognized as an important part of psychosocial rehabilitation (Clarke et al., 2009). Indeed, it is already known that when goals are clearly specified, people are more likely to reach them (Locke and Latham, 1990; cited in Clarke et al., 2009). In the collaborative goal-striving process, however, there is an inclusion of a recovery vision process that aims to clarify the person's values and dreams. These are then linked to short-term goals. Discussing and agreeing on a person's vision for recovery is a mechanism by which the individual's need for a meaningful life is incorporated into the treatment planning (Andresen et al., 2003). The attempt here is to make goals both attainable and meaningful. The clinician's role in this process is to guide the person through the process – to provide a therapeutic relationship in which there is sufficient trust for the person to be able to discuss what is meaningful, purposeful and valued to them in terms of how they would like their life to be. It is also about helping to align shorter-term goals to build into and be thematically truthful to their personal recovery vision.

Evidence-based coaching

There is a significant shift in focus for the development of mental health professional expertise towards one of psychological 'coach'. Coaching psychology is a relatively nascent field (Green et al., 2006; Grant and Cavanagh, 2007). Early controlled trials indicate that using a cognitive-behavioural, solution-focused, life-coaching, group-based programme can lead to statistically significant differences in increased striving towards goals, improved subjective well-being, psychological well-being and hope (Green et al., 2006). This study examined the impact of a life-coaching programme on a non-clinical participant sample of 56 adults completing self-report measures prior to the group programme, at the completion of the group programme and at 20, 30 and 40 weeks thereafter. There is then some early emerging evidence from this study and from other similar controlled studies that such coaching techniques can produce a sustained effect on these positive-psychological measures, albeit in a non-clinical sample of participants. Clearly there is a need to reproduce such experiments, with a greater deal of rigour, with participants experiencing psychosis. There is some preliminary evidence, however, that when this approach is implemented into secondary mental health care services, service-users find that staff increasingly use evidence-based goal-setting principles in the delivery of their care (Clarke et al., 2009).

The collaborative recovery model

An implementation of recovery-focused coaching – as in a solution-focused, cognitive-behavioural model as described by Green and colleagues (2006) – is elaborated and has been further developed and evaluated in parts by Oades and fellows (2009). Their collaborative recovery model has been constructed to be consistent with the current expert consensus of recovery-focused practice and to promote person-centred and strengths-focused practice (Oades et al., 2009). The guiding principles of the CRM are as outlined in Table 5.4.

These fundamental principles have been developed into a staff-coaching programme, and implicit within this developmental attitude-challenging programme is a normalizing assumption that we all have, irregardless of mental health status, strengths, values, goals and the need for the development of a growth focus (Couley and Oades, 2007). A realization here is that the organization delivering the development of recovery-focused approaches also needs to go through a recovery process of its own – transforming from an organization primarily preoccupied with treatment-based, expert-staff/novice–patient relationships to a collaborative partnership model of care delivery (Couley and Oades, 2007).

Part of this organizational recovery process involves overcoming certain 'institutional resistances' to change (Davidson et al., 2006). One of these that is common to organizations implementing a recovery-focused model is an institutional concern about risk. A more collaborative, recovery-focused model supports the autonomy of the patient or service-user: there is a real committed focus on empowerment and self-management. This can raise concerns amongst clinicians that there is increased risk taking on the part of service-users and organizations with concomitant liability issues (Oades et al., 2009). This is a barrier raised by organizations with a traditional risk-aversive care approach. A fundamental issue, then, might be that staff attitudes and values may change and align with the recovery agenda [as is evident from the research of Crowe and colleagues (2006)] but that the implementation of recovery-focused practice into clinical action remains hampered by

Table 5.4 Fundamental components of the CRM model (taken from Oades et al., 2009)

Guiding principle 1	Recovery is an individual process
Guiding principle 2	Collaboration and autonomy support
Component 1	Change enhancement
Component 2	Strengths and values clarification
Component 3	Collaborative vision and goal striving
Component 4	Collaborative action planning and monitoring

resistant traditional practices. It is thus imperative in the development of recovery-focused practice training programmes that there are measures of 'fidelity' used to evaluate the implementation of practice. It is also imperative that change occurs throughout the organization – top-down and bottom-up for a whole-organization change.

Early study findings on the impact of the CRM model as applied in practice are that consumers evaluate the service they receive as being more consistent with the espoused recovery model. Specifically, they find that they are more often encouraged by staff to take responsibility for their recovery and that there is an increased collaboration with their staff service provider, as well as increased application of goal setting and homework in their day-to-day care (Marshall et al., 2009; Clarke et al., 2009).

Evidence for recovery education programmes: Recovery colleges

There is a dearth of research on the effectiveness of so-called recovery colleges or recovery education programmes. Here, clinical practice seems ahead of recovery research because there is a rapid growth in the development of recovery colleges in the UK. This has emerged out of the ImROC (Implementing Recovery Organizational Change) programme, which seeks to address the 'organizational challenges' of implementing recovery practice (Perkins and Slade, 2012). One of the few studies of recovery education programmes (Dunn et al., 2008) implemented a quasi experimental study of a recovery programme derived from the empirical literature and built upon earlier findings that recovery-oriented illness management can reduce symptoms, reduce relapse and improve quality of life (Mueser et al., 2002).

Dunn and colleagues' (2008) study looked at an educationally immersed programme of recovery-focused education. Measures of the experience of symptoms, distress, self-concept, quality of life, empowerment and recovery attitude were repeated throughout the study (Dunn et al., 2008). The centre offered courses on physical health (e.g. tai chi, nutrition), personal development (e.g. journaling, peer support training, recovery workshops, wellness recovery action planning), employment (e.g. career planning, coping at work, office skills) and education (e.g. Internet use, introduction to computer use, writing seminars).

Participants in the programme had a diagnosis of some kind of 'serious and persistent mental illness' and met with an advisor to choose up to four courses each semester. These were weekly classes for 12 weeks, with three 12-week semesters per calendar year. Attendance rates were high; on average, each participant attended 110 hours of classes with an average attendance per course of 60%. Teachers were a mix of mental health service-users and subject-specialist instructors (16 of 26 were service-users). All of the teachers were given weekly group and individual supervision on skills teaching and providing support to people with mental health difficulties in an educational milieu.

Bearing in mind the normal caveats regarding research studies, the outcomes of Dunn and colleagues' (2008) study indicated that, on both phobic anxiety and interpersonal sensitivity scales, there was a significant reduction in distress over time above that of the comparison group. There were trends of experiencing less distress around paranoia and psychotism that did not reach statistical significance. There was a non-significant trend also towards an improvement of emotional well-being. There was a significant improvement for the experimental group in quality of life, empowerment, support and affirmation and recovery scales.

Beyond the recovery college delivery studies of 'relapse prevention' programmes, which teach stress management skills and working with individualized early warning signs of relapse, have all showed decreases in relapse and rehospitalization (Mueser et al., 2002). Programmes of 'coping skills training' as a means of 'illness management' have consistently demonstrated effectiveness in reducing symptom severity (Mueser et al., 2002).

Paradigmatic change in evidence and research

Whilst the development of recovery-oriented practice demands a significant shift in collaboration and the locus of control in decision making and care, the same could also be said of the needs of service-users in relation to that of research. In order to bring an empirical lens to the notion of recovery and in this sense validate the adoption of the approach to existing mental health organizations, academics and researchers have had to engage in a significant period of in-depth qualitative research. This has enabled conceptual frameworks of recovery as evident within Oades and colleagues' (2009) and Slade and fellows' (2011) research programmes into the Collaborative Recovery Model and REFOCUS. 'Consumer research' or 'User Research' is a process whereby not only are the experiences of service-users (i.e. it is the experience of the person that is the subject of the research), but also the collaboration of the service-user in the research process itself is sought to some greater or lesser degree. Just as clinical practice seeks to 'involve' service-users in care and is perhaps slowly shifting towards recognizing that involvement in of itself must transform more into a collaborative/partnership approach to avoid tokenism and marginalization, so research and education are also recognizing the need for active, collaborative service-user research. In some areas, this has led to participant-researchers being employed specifically to support processes of the research programme, such as helping to create and validate evaluative and measurement tools (e.g. Marshall, 2008), and to entire service-user-led research projects (e.g. Rose et al., 2011).

Research is increasingly recognizing the need to draw upon the expertise of service-users and apply, in some sense, the recovery model onto itself. Without a significant shift, however, in the status of lived experience or personal testimony, as well as the recognition of the value of this within professional clinical–researcher communities, these kinds of use–research integrations run the risk of tokenism. The use of a balanced mixed-method approach in research programmes is beginning to flourish. Yet within research circles, the dominance of quantitative paradigms as the gold standards of research continues. This has been particularly clear in the recent debate in academic and research circles in a variety of social media forums on the efficacy of Cognitive-Behavioural Therapy (CBT) for psychosis, where the application of user accounts and experiences of using the therapy have been (to summarize some of the online professional debate) derided as 'anecdata' (Kings College London, 2013).

Whilst there are no doubt good historical reasons for being cautious over the empirical status of such an 'introspectionist' account, there is also no doubt that collectively the experiences of people with psychosis and recovery can constitute valuable material for developing effective interventions. This is evident from current research work into recovery as summarized here. It is also a potentially stigmatizing and 'othering' process to trivialize the value of such experiences. An approach that seeks to integrate and contextualize the qualitative accounts of participants in health care research is that of meta-synthesis.

This qualitative approach is akin to meta-analysis in quantitative research, and there has been a marked increase in the appearance of meta-synthesis papers in nursing and psychology literature in the past ten years. This process seeks to integrate the accounts of participants from different but interrelated qualitative research papers and has come under some fire amongst interpretivist researchers in particular, who point out that attempting to summarize collections of qualitative accounts runs counter to the principles of constructivist meaning-making approaches to knowledge (Campbell et al., 2003). No doubt various strands of relatively pure meta-synthesis methodologies will differentiate and emerge as this nascent field of qualitative research approach evolves. There is something appealing in the idea of being able to gaze upon a body of people's sense-making of given experiences and phenomena, if not as a robust theory, then at least as a window behind the perceptual curtain of subjective experience.

Conclusions

Research into recovery, then, is poised at an interesting point. It seeks to develop a call, from service-user and survivor accounts, for acknowledgement, first, that hope of recovery is real and that people do recover, in a broad variety of senses, from so-called mental illness. Second, this recovery movement also calls for a change in the nature of mental health treatment – towards empowering, collaborative experiences that support the individual to learn to adapt to their experience and grow beyond – but also to be supported into a meaningful life within the context of this recovery. Academic and scientific research as an interpreter of service-user wishes stands between such survivor/service-user wishes and accounts and clinical practice. There is a considerable risk of the recovery becoming yet another 're-branding' of services and appropriated within the established traditional treatment model. This is something that is clearly acknowledged within research's approaches to recovery. It has spawned the recognition of the need for true partnership in the service delivery, evaluation and research processes. There is naturally something of a potential gap between the recognition of this need and acting upon it in both clinical and research terms.

Slade and colleagues (2014) explicitly address the potential for recovery to become another means by which the provision of mental health care is subject to professional and organizational 'abuse', explicitly or implicitly, through a loss in translation or a distortion of implementation. This foreshadows Chapter 7 of this volume, which seeks to explore, from a political perspective, the rich but also equally dark possibilities of recovery.

Recovery from a research perspective has service-user accounts and lived experience at its very heart, albeit seen through the potentially distorting translational lenses of academic and clinical researchers. The inclusion of service-users in the research process – if done to a meaningful and respectful degree – has the potential to obviate some of these concerns if undertaken with an underpinning notion of partnership and collaboration. Merely including service-users' voices within focus group exercises is, I would argue, insufficient and tantamount to professional tokenism. A spectrum that emphasizes the development and legitimacy of professional peer-research is needed – nothing else is sufficient or acceptable – if the recovery-based approach is serious about its own foundations and principles.

There is some preliminarily encouraging evidence that principles espoused within recovery processes are fruitful and useful for both service-providers and participant-consumers alike. It is leading to the developing of potentially very innovative services. Robust evaluation and safeguarding the participant-user's voice within the implementation and activities of the organization are clearly imperative for recovery not only to survive but also to thrive and flourish into a productive means of providing nurturing services that can facilitate people's growth through the experience of psychosis and beyond.

Chapter 6

Recovery, psychosis and identity

This chapter seeks to review the role that a person's identity has to play both in the experience of psychosis itself and in the process of recovery. First, the idea of identity will be defined, discussed and critiqued. Second, the relationship between identity and related concepts within the experience of psychosis will be explored. Third, the interplay of identity and recovery will be examined. Throughout this discussion, reference to lived experience and empirical research will be applied within overarching post-modernist and trans-modernist frameworks as appropriate.

What is identity?

Identity is a rather poorly explicated term that has been co-opted for a variety of purposes and put to use in many contexts. Coming from the Latin *idem* meaning 'the same', it implies that identity is something both uniquely individual to the person and yet also somehow nominatively consistent over time (Buckingham, 2008). Identity then in part refers to characteristics or stable components of our 'self' but is also attached to wider notions of collective groups – hence national identity, cultural identity and gender identity as examples. Here, then, lies a philosophical but also highly pragmatic tension: how can one struggle to be 'true to oneself' (i.e. strive for personal authenticity) whilst seeking a sense of identity and belonging within larger social groups. Who a person is, as well as being a product of their narrative biographical history, is also influenced by their social context and situation amongst a number of other things (Buckingham, 2008). Identity is also a topic that has been embraced by a wide variety of scientific disciplines, each bringing elements of their specific discipline to the concept of identity.

Psychology for example has brought a variety of understandings across its subdisciplines to the study of identity. The narrative approach upholds the idea that severe mental illness can be a threat to narrative agency in that it can obstruct the person's capacity to be the "author of one's own narrative" (Carless, 2008, p. 10). Third-wave contextualized psychotherapies often emphasize the need to develop a so-called meaningful life. In some sense, given what we know of psychosis, this makes a great deal of sense as a potential restorative action.

Recall the meta-synthesis of McCarthy-Jones and colleagues (2013) introduced in Chapter 3. Psychosis, amongst other things, involves the loss of consensual world-understanding. An early part of recovery in psychosis is the reconciliation of this. Quite frequently, it also entails a great deal of other losses – the loss of roles and functions, particularly a loss of security in self and relationships, and oft-times periods of loss of liberty as a result of enforced treatment. It is ironic that at a time when a person can typically feel most unsure about themselves and the validity of their very self-experience, the mainstay of treatment involves taking them away from their own environment and possible supportive relationships. It also involves keeping them at a distance from the world, often at a time when there is already a lack of security in a sense of place in the world. Naturally, this could well be beneficial if the 'treating' environment is therapeutic and the period of treatment well timed. Prolonged periods of inpatient treatment, however, can lead to institutionalization and social disablement. Rebuilding a sense of self and security with self and world through meaningful and purposeful activities turns out to be a key recovery intervention.

A critical factor perhaps in successfully leveraging any therapeutic interventions for recovery is this finding of meaning and relevance. This is naturally highly individually subjective – what I might find meaningful and relevant to my life may well prove of little value to yours. It is thus essential to focus attention on the individual's personal life history and sociocultural context when it comes to understanding the mechanisms of their recovery (Carless, 2008). It is the contention of narrative psychology that what is at the heart of being is the ability to create a story of our lives as an essential structure to self (Bruner, 1986). Telling a story of your life is an element believed to be essential for maintaining the integrity and consistency of self (Crossley, 2000).

The experience of psychosis itself, as well as the impact of being identified as a person with an illness, can have a 'dehumanizing' effect on the person (Dilks et al., 2010). This can be reinforced by unhelpful effects from medication, particularly weight gain and sexual dysfunction, that can impact on self-identity and self-esteem (Laithwaite and Gumley, 2007). It is also possible that clinicians can damage the person's self-esteem (Bassett et al., 2001) by treating them as a 'disordered' person with an undue focus on symptoms, treatment and illness. It is vital therefore that mental health services adjust their focus to the wider context of the person. The loss of meaningful activities is particularly damaging to the person's esteem and sense of self, and a focus on simply having a job can be of vital importance to regaining or rebuilding these lost components (Wagner and King, 2005). One of the ways this seems to be so valuable to people recovering from psychosis is that it can lead to finding a sense of security in the world (Campbell and Morrison, 2007).

Getting back to work or finding an alternative source of work can often first be aided by assisting with social recovery (Gee et al., 2003). Supporting the person in repairing relationships that may have been damaged – by the person's behaviour whilst experiencing psychosis, or from the impact of unwanted effects of drugs, or through difficulties in communicating through both of these – is a vital step to help people feel more secure with themselves and with others (Redmond et al., 2010). Factors contributing to regaining social relationships include routine, medication, spirituality and religion (McCarthy-Jones et al., 2013). Experiencing relationships with mental health professionals can scaffold this by having a person demonstrate a willingness to understand their experiences, be non-judgemental and demonstrate consistency (McCarthy-Jones et al., 2013). An important factor cited within rebuilding the self is developing a de-centred, non-judgemental relationship with the experiences of psychosis itself, for example heard voices (Chin et al., 2009).

A key to understanding these kinds of experience from a psychological perspective is to embrace the idea that such unusual experiences are part of an attempt on the person to make sense of their experience (Maher, 1988). For instance ambiguous social information and anomalous bodily sensations are often combined in the formation of persecutory paranoid beliefs (Freeman and Garety, 2006). So for example a person might be feeling odd and anxious and rather than thinking, 'I'm feeling pretty stressed and anxious here – I've lost a lot of sleep lately', interpret their experience as, 'These people are looking at me oddly – they are out to harm me'. Feelings of irritation or anger, in combination with anxiety, are perhaps particularly ripe emotional materials for persecutory ideas to form as an explanation for these sensations (Freeman and Garety, 2006).

Freeman and colleagues' (2006) approach to working with paranoid thoughts is to support the person to become a more detached observer of their fears. They are encouraged not to fight with suspicious thoughts when they happen and to focus on what they are doing rather than on what they are thinking. This is combined with reviewing the evidence underpinning paranoid interpretations and fostering the capacity to develop more flexible alternative lines of thought. On top of this, meta-cognitive approaches to decrease the amount of time spent worrying about paranoid thoughts is added in using a Metacognitive Therapy (MCT) approach (Wells, 2009).

This approach foreshadows, in some relational areas, the subsequent work of applying Mindfulness to the experience of psychosis by Chadwick and colleagues (2005, 2009). This approach combines an initial Mindful breathing intervention to ground the person's awareness to their body and breath (Chadwick et al., 2005, 2009). Guidance by the practitioner is frequent during the Mindfulness meditation to reduce the possibility of the person becoming entangled with ruminating upon their experience. It is supported by a group reflection on the experience of the process, using guided discovery to help the participants voice their findings and experience of the process. The process of developing Mindfulness skills is intended to help the person learn that their cognitive-behavioural reactions to the experience can lead to increased distress and that feared consequences of not adhering to these maintaining behaviours are not borne out during moments of Mindfulness. This encourages the dropping of such initially short-term safety seeking but ultimately longer-term distress-enhancing behaviours. This is what Chadwick and fellows (2005, 2009) refer to as the development of 'choiceless awareness' in the face of such experiences.

Abba and colleagues (2008) undertook a grounded theory analysis of participants learning to apply Mindfulness to their experiences. The participants described a process of learning to let go of attempts to get rid of or to avoid difficult experiences, instead allowing them to come into awareness, whilst letting go of fighting, judgement and promoting acceptance of both the experience and the self. Results from early trials of these interventions are encouraging in that they are well tolerated and lead to significant improvement in clinical functioning and in Mindfulness of distressing thoughts and images (Chadwick et al., 2005, 2009; Langer et al., 2012).

Narrative theory, self and recovery

Psychology, particularly over the last 30 or so years, has become heavily influenced by social constructionist approaches, and this has led to the development of so-called narrative psychology approaches (Crossley, 2000). Social constructionism emphasizes the importance of linguistic and cultural aspects of the experience of self, identity and relationships with others (Crossley, 2000). Traditionalist, or more 'realist', psychological approaches to identity presume that the 'self' exists as a measurable entity that can be discovered and described. Constructionist approaches, in contrast, sees the self as necessarily embedded within social and cultural language and assumes that this is subject to considerable change and variation over time. Indeed, some theorists claim that the rise of language as a representational medium is itself responsible for the phenomenological experience of consciousness (Jaynes, 1976; Fodor, 1976).

The capacity to reflexively think about oneself is perhaps a core ingredient of human experience (Crossley, 2000). In narrative psychology, another central component is the experience of time in meaning-making (Crossley, 2000). Narrative psychology holds that human experience involves a sense of continuity of experience over time that involves a sense of order or sequence. Another characteristic feature is that of connectedness or relatedness to others, and this is also an essential source of structure in our search for meaning. To some narrative theorists, the essence of identity is inevitably incorporated in how an individual draws significance from events (Taylor, 1989). This means that our values, which help us identify what constitutes a worthwhile life, are necessarily fundamental to our self-experience for they help inform what constitutes a significant-to-us life event.

Theorists such as Dennett (1991), to some greater or lesser degree, hold that the nature of human experience is contained within its storytelling. For example we attend a social gathering. At this event, someone we don't know particularly well practically ignores us. What sense we make of this depends on our interpretation of events. We might think that this person has something specifically against 'us' ('They don't like us'), and we can enter into a self–other narrative with a paranoid theme, or we might bring a sense-making interpretation ('They're anxious around other people – they don't want to be here') that leads to an entirely different strand of experience. Disruption to our narrative coherency via trauma often also involves a radical re-conceptualization of self, others and world (Crossley, 2000). Narrative reconfiguration is a process whereby people adapt to trauma through a process of rebuilding a sense of security and renewed sense of meaning in the experience (Crossley, 2000).

The 'illness' identity and recovery model

Yanos and colleagues (2010) propose a model that seeks to identify the role of the relationship with the 'illness' in the course of recovery. Note here the use of scare-quotes. Not all will find the idea of illness to be a useful framework for discussing their experiences. In the course of the experience of psychosis, a person may experience a range of new life experiences with a degree of challenge and difficulty attached. For example they may hear voices, or have beliefs that are unusual to some degree or other to themselves and/or others. They may struggle in their lives or work, and this may lead them to need support. To some degree or other, often as a result of interaction with others and professional services, the person attaches an interpretation of 'illness' to some of their experiences.

Of course a person may reject such an identity; however, this will not necessarily lead to a more productive relationship with services and will not stop professional services from ascribing the illness identity to the person. In a sense, there is a socially mediated narrative process in the construction of mental illness identity formation. Internalizing negative stereotypes of 'mental illness' can result in an additional experience of depression (Birchwood et al., 1993). It's also worth noting that in their study of the experience of depression, Birchwood and colleagues (1993) found that in people with chronic psychosis, the perception of how controllable their psychotic experiences were was a means of discriminating between incidence of depression or non-depression.

Following Yanos and fellows' (2010) model, once awareness of the other-imposed illness identity or in some cases the self-imposed illness identity is acknowledged, a variety of consequential meanings are assigned. A person might for instance believe that they are weak because of the presence of an illness. Such attached beliefs have the potential to impact upon hope and self-esteem, self-esteem being the way in which one evaluates the self (Yanos et al., 2010). Here, following narrative theory, we have not only the experience of the illness itself but also a parallel process of interpreting what having that experience means to the person and as a consequence what this says about the person. What kinds of beliefs are attached are also subject to sociocultural moderation. Heightened expectations of dangerousness and violence, as well as the belief that a person with such a history cannot sustain employment, are common unhelpful and misleading societal views (Martin et al., 2000).

Hopefulness and self-esteem, as we already know from our survey of recovery research in Chapter 4, are essential components of successful recovery. A lack of these can lead to depressive reactions and increase the risk of self-harm and suicide. Yanos and colleagues (2010) hypothesize that subsequent coping actions will be shaped by such beliefs and mediated by hopefulness and self-regard. The coping actions will vary in their adaptability and will in turn serve to moderate and mediate ongoing unusual or 'psychotic' experiences. Some generally supportive evidence exists for this model. For example Roe's (2001) longitudinal qualitative study of recovery from severe mental illness found that people who improve in functioning over a year-long period showed development in their identity from 'patient' to 'person' – that is maintaining a 'patient' identity can be detrimental to recovery. Many longitudinal case studies suggest that initial steps are reclamation of self-agency (Lysaker et al., 2005, 2007). Participating in so-called consumer-run organizations – set up by and run by people diagnosed with mental illness that set out to provide self-help, peer support and similar services – can scaffold recovery by encouraging participants through self-disclosure and advocacy to transform themselves towards personhood and less stigmatizing identities (Yanos et al., 2010).

Studies have found more specific evidence for other aspects of the 'illness identity' model. Namely, that there is a relationship between internalizing negative stigmatic messages and lowered self-esteem and hope (Watson et al., 2007). The degree to which a person holds the belief that others have negative, devaluing and discriminatory beliefs about the 'mentally ill' is related again to lowered self-esteem and a decreased sense of agency (Link et al., 2001; Wright et al., 2000; cited in Yanos et al., 2010). These kinds of findings are noteworthy for mental health professionals who have an empirically driven mandate to provide hope, challenge societal stigma and support people in avoiding self-stigma.

There is evidence that the personal evaluations of coping actions has the hypothesized directional effect on the experience of 'symptoms'. Strous and colleagues (2005) for example found that changes in ways of coping are associated with changes in the severity of symptoms over time. Randomized trials of supported employment (Bond et al., 2001) have shown that people with severe mental health difficulties participating in 'competitive work' show greater rates of improvement in contrast with those who don't engage in such programmes. Clearly, in the development of recovery-focused services, explicitly developing services that set out to work with the impact of the development of identity relations with 'illness experiences' is necessary. Tailoring 'treatment' to align with the individual's idiosyncratic meaning-making, to best leverage the development of self-agency, hope and self-regard in conjunction with opportunities to access appropriately supported work programmes, has the potential to support significant personal recovery. Embedding this within consumer-led service development, as in the recovery college model, also has the potential to leverage gains in movements towards enabling-identity forms. However, all of these kinds of recovery-focused developments must be developed with strong partnership and collaboration with those seeking to use the services and are as prone to misuse and abuse as other forms of traditional treatment (see Chapter 7 for more on the political dangers of recovery).

Recovery, identity and the social role

Recovery and personal identity, then, is a dominant theme in the current climate of mental health services and is often conceptualized as requiring shifts in attitudes and values (Repper and Perkins, 2003). It is also associated with growth and learning (Bonney and Stickley, 2008). It is clear from the development of the recovery movement that these recovery processes do not occur in a social vacuum; indeed quite the opposite, recovery seems to necessitate establishing a valued social role as a means of claiming a positive personal identity (Royal College of Psychiatrists, Care Services Improvement Partnership and Social Care Institute for Excellence, 2007). It is one of the dangers of positivistic approaches to mental health discourse that empirical research has focused overly on the deficits within individuals as simultaneously the source of mental health problems and the focus of treatment. It is also a risk in defining recovery as an 'individual's' process or journey that we may overlook the importance of social infrastructure.

In their systematic literature review, Tew and fellows (2012) explored the relevant factors that served to enhance social recovery. This included the adoption of a strengths-based approach as part of a process of supporting the "transformation from an illness-dominated identity to an identity of agency [and] competence" (Mancini, 2007, p. 50). Self-directed support is another mechanism that can facilitate empowerment. A practical means of services supporting this can be seen in the development of personal budgets. The early outcomes of national pilots of such schemes in the UK have established that people find themselves more involved in decision making about their care – more in control as a result and able to exercise greater choice (Tew et al., 2012).

Successful stigma resistance seems to depend, at least in part, on developing and sustaining positive social relationships outside the mental health system (Tew et al., 2012). Indeed, the mental health system may be an active barrier to maintaining such relationships with the processes of risk management and assessment, hospitalization, ghetto-like social housing arrangements and so forth. Along with these effective, targeted anti-stigma actions can help prevent 'othering' in communities by providing opportunities for people to have prolonged personal contact with the potentially stigmatized other, to have dialogue with them and to hear their personal stories. These seem to be the core ingredients of interventions that tackle attitudinal change (Pinfold et al., 2005).

Services thus need to develop clarity over how they can support users to enhance their connectedness with others in a way that is commensurate with their capacity to cope and indeed benefit from such relationships. In the earlier phase of recovery, there is now a recognition of how workers should adopt a stance of 'standing alongside' and 'being with' the person. There is less known about how to move productively to accelerate the development of autonomy and agency for the person; further qualitative research is required for these important aspects of social recovery.

MY LIVED EXPERIENCE OF RECOVERY: THE ART OF REFORGING THE SELF IN SOCIETY

Looking back over my own recovery, within the limits of retrospective reflective review, I can acknowledge certain factors that contributed to this success. Firstly, paradoxically, the lack of meaningful support from community mental health services with regard to my ongoing treatment was a factor. I was frustrated at living a life, on medication, seemingly forever in a sheltered housing environment. At this point, whilst life was considerably better than it had been on the ward (and a relatively brief and turgid spell in a 'rehabilitation unit' in the middle of nowhere), it was hardly an inspiring and mind-stretching experience. Bear in mind that, prior to this emotional and psychological collapse, I had had a promising academic career in, ironically, psychological science.

The lack of recovery-focused support from services effectively created a vacuum I felt obliged to fill myself. What I wanted was a meaningful and satisfying life – and what I had within the services of the time was a begrudgingly subsidized existence. I began with some voluntary work and started to systematically reduce my use of medications (see Chapter 4). In terms of the conceptual framework of recovery proposed by Leamy and colleagues (2011), for me at that time, it was the frustration and lack of satisfaction with components of the Meaning category that galvanized my recovery socially. The unwavering social support I had from my network of friends constituted something of a social Rogerian-style network; they were non-judgemental, consistent, authentic and, when necessary, empathetic (Rogers, 1980). They also provided a place to be 'me' without endless questions or discussions as to how I was feeling or what was wrong or up with me or what medication I should be on and how much. In other words, there was a focus on life goals rather than on treatment goals in this informal form of caring support.

There was certainly a sustained phase wherein I was very angry at the care (or lack of it) I had received and was receiving from services, as well as anger at having gone through such painful, strange and seemingly irrevocably damaging experiences. In terms of Chadwick's (2005) model, I was very much 'caught up' with my experiences and had yet to develop acceptance and psychological flexibility around them. It was only through seeking to 'get on with life' and learning to enjoy the here and now of what I was doing that I started to develop the capacity to accept what had happened to me. In a sense, I engaged in the social aspects of recovery that acted as a kind of Mindfully supportive environment to me.

In a sense, these are processes that correspond to the ideas of narrative theory. In order to get back into life because my experience was of a service that was preoccupied with treatment, it was necessary for me to circumnavigate care because it was entrenching me into services that were more about 'containing' and 'stabilizing' than taking positive risks to further growth. Naturally, I had concerns about being able to make it and a dread of a relapse and everything that relapse implied. Particularly, the thought of needing to return to inpatient treatment was a barrier to taking risks in terms of my social recovery. Ultimately, I couldn't just remain satisfied with the voluntary work I did in the charity sector. Whilst it was helpful in terms of my getting into a routine and feeling to some extent that I was doing something helpful (if not exactly in alignment with how I wanted my life to be), it was never going to be anything other than a stepping stone to test my capacity to withstand stress and develop confidence in my self-security.

Having gone from experiences that had left me feeling very insecure in the world – with my experience but also with how others related to me – reforging a sense of confidence in my own resilience was a vital recovery step. I use the term 'reforging' here most deliberately: making something stronger anew but also testing its durability and reliability in the stressful environment of real-world experience (Stevenson, 2010). Without particularly planning it, I undertook a series of tests of my self-confidence and resilience by trying out for college courses, signing off sickness benefit and onto job seekers allowance, going for job interviews and doing various forms of work. Getting signed up to a temping agency was a particularly good thing for me; I could get relatively decently paid work, try out different places of work and jobs, all without signing up for too long a commitment to any one thing. This ultimately led me to take a more permanent position for several years that, in turn, led me to retrain from psychology into nursing and the beginning of my current professional career. Identity is undoubtedly, in my experience, a significant component of recovery but, without attendant status and the possibility of regaining such through meaningful and socially valued activity, it is hard to reforge your identity.

A barrier to recovery: Legitimized knowledge

A significant challenge to the rise of recovery is in asserting the validity and utility of different kinds of knowledge. Psychiatry has legitimized the power of professional and scientific knowledge. This places the knowledge of the individual significantly further down the empirical ladder than knowledge uncovered by research organizations. This is what Foucault referred to as 'popular knowledges' (Foucault, 1980) and is also referred to, in parallel, in the philosophy of mind literature as 'folk psychology' or 'naïve psychology' (Churchland, 1988). It is also a challenge to the claim that psychiatry and indeed psychology are scientific disciplines. As Corbin and Strauss (2008) have pointed out, can we consider a discipline a valid science that systematically ignores or sidelines a source of knowledge as insignificant or unimportant?

A barrier to therapeutic relationships: 'Professionalism'

Recovery research identifies that the therapeutic relationship between user and professional is a significant vehicle within which healing occurs. Most of our understanding about the nature of therapeutic relationships has been under the banner of psychotherapeutic research that largely has been struggling to disprove the so-called dodo bird effect. This effect is the hypothesis that the method of psychotherapeutic treatment is secondary to the helping alliance that it is contained within (Budd and Hughes, 2009).

People recovering from psychosis and other severe mental health difficulties have identified a number of factors in relationships with professionals that have supported their recovery. One of these is that the relationship is, to some extent or other, reciprocal. This is an area in which a significant barrier to developing such a helpful aspect of working alliance is professionalism or professional boundaries. Reciprocity can come from the professional asking the service-user for help for example or from extending the duration of a visit beyond regular service hours. These kinds of actions establish that the person is more than a mere patient (Davidson and Strauss, 1992). However, they are likely to be associated with a disregard for professional values and prohibited to some degree or other by the professional's organizational institution. In a sense, a focus on recovery values and placing the person's experiences centre stage in eliciting the important components of recovery afford us the opportunity to challenge the orthodoxy of one-dimensional sources of knowledge. The established practices and vision of the mental health professional is also included as something that necessitates recovery.

Conclusions

For all its contextual vagaries, the idea of identity is clearly a critical component in understanding recovery and the obstacles to it. It suggests a variety of means and levels through which people can influence their relationship with distressing experiences and foster the development of a meaningful and worthwhile life. Attending to the role of identity affords us insights into how recovery-focused practice can seek to scaffold recovery at a variety of levels – individually, interrelationally, communally and therapeutically. Focusing on the role of identity in recovery also highlights to us the signal dangers of attending to dominant strands of knowledge construction and adds flesh to Grant's (2009) call for paradigmatic pluralism encountered earlier in Chapter 2.

Chapter 7

Political dimensions of recovery

This chapter seeks to identify and discuss some of the relevant political dimensions of recovery. This involves a review of the situational context of recovery-focused practice, in terms of the professional and organizational milieu in which recovery-focused services are delivered. It will also explore the wider organizational context – namely the governmental. This will be explored from an empirical and critical post-modernist stance as appropriate.

What do we mean by the 'politics' of recovery?

Recovery as a 'movement' is a banner under which it is possible for professionals, service-users and allied stakeholders to gather and collaborate in the transformation and delivery of mental health services (Roberts and Wolfson, 2004). It is not specifically 'anti-psychiatry', although a pro-recovery movement does hold challenges that could readily be perceived as such, particularly with regard to the handling of risk and the use of a partnership decision-making approach. There is a challenge to the holding of decision-making power inherent in the recovery approach.

Recovery itself is a concept that is vulnerable to abuses by all – professionals, governmental organizations, radicals and service-users (Slade et al., 2014). An understandable early concern of proponents of recovery is that it may become distorted in adoption by professional organizations (Slade et al., 2014). It is thus worthwhile, considering the 'politics' of recovery and the potential barriers and pitfalls of organizational attempts to implement recovery. Recovery should not turn out to be yet another thing 'done' to people with mental health difficulties or used as leverage against service-users if they fail to meet organizationally set goals or outcomes.

Potential abuses of recovery: Organizational obstacles and resistance

Shifting clinical practice to be truly founded upon partnership in decision making, with an emphasis on realistic hope of recovery, challenges orthodox professional practice to let go of power and authority within their customary roles and practice (Slade et al., 2014). This is no small challenge in and of itself, and, given also that there are some legal frameworks such as the Mental Health Act (1983/2007) that afford powers in certain circumstances of detention and enforced treatment, it is perhaps hard to see how services can maintain a recovery approach when these powers are at play. As a social justice movement working in partnership with professionals to deliberate over appropriate legal reform, the recovery movement has a larger agenda to address.

At the heart of this is the erroneous and indeed to some extent the highly toxic idea that recovery is something that can be supported through a combination of increasingly effective and in places legally enforced treatment (Slade et al., 2014). Community treatment orders (CTOs) in the UK were introduced as a means of reducing the need for admission and detention in inpatient settings. The data on the rates of admission and implementation of CTOs do not support these ideas, and neither do early randomized trials evaluating the efficacy of CTOs. According to the Health and Social Care Information Centre (2009, 2013), rates of detention to inpatient facilities in the UK increased from 47,600 in 2007/2008 – 2008 being the year in which CTOs were introduced – to 50,408 in 2012/2013. Within the limitations of designing and implementing RCTs (randomized controlled trials), those conducted to investigate the efficacy of CTOs in reducing the need for admission to hospital each unequivocally indicate that CTOs do not have an impact statistically on such outcomes (Burns and Molodynski, 2014). There is in counterbalance to this some evidence that the use of CTOs can reduce the length of hospital stay for certain groups of people (Light, 2014).

As Light (2014) points out in discussing the whys and wherefores of the legitimacy of CTOs in the face of unfolding contradictory and in places unequivocally negative evidence, the process of study design, the choice of 'outcomes measures' and what kinds of evidence inform evidence-based care are philosophical matters. An implication of such studies thus far on CTOs is that inpatient treatment in some sense is the result of a failure of the CTO; that is there is an assumption that the function of community care is to prevent the need for inpatient treatment. In a clinical context, this does not always make particularly good sense;

sometimes the purpose of community mental health care is to *facilitate* access to inpatient care. It has also been argued that CTOs, like recovery, amounts to a process – wherein the benefit entailed within the treatment order is in the improved access and availability of clinical resources to the person (Kisely et al., 2013). The nuances of measurement as a factor in the accrual of evidence and legitimacy of certain kinds of practice is discussed in more detail in Chapter 8.

These studies also fail to speak to the qualitative nature of experiencing a CTO; the most recent studies of which in Australia (Light, 2014) paint a consistent picture of distress and ambivalence about the use of CTOs there. Strangely, whilst studies of lived experience or qualitative data tend to have a reduced regard in terms of health-economic decision making where randomized trials are seen as the gold standard for research, a rebuttal of the OCTET (Oxford Community Treatment Order Evaluation Trial) evidence by Mustafa (2013) argues against the withdrawal of CTOs based largely on a fictitious what-if scenario of how CTOs could be useful! We are well overdue embracing mixed methodologies in psychological health 'science' and finding ways to draw upon user experiences so that we can provide interventions that are both empirically valid and experientially attentive.

Mental health professionals are often unhelpfully preoccupied with the idea that recovery is a process whereby, through diagnosis and treatment, people are cured of their symptoms (Slade et al., 2014). This is, as discussed in some detail in Chapter 2, a rather limited view and interpretation of what recovery means. It is also a view that often entails lifelong application of treatment and the threat of 'underlying illnesses' relapsing courtesy of significant life stressors. It is one of the reasons that 'recovery' as a banner label is unhelpful because of its deep-rooted medical connotations. The shift in UK policy to provide systems of mental health care that enable personal recovery demands that services not only provide access to appropriate (and preferably effective and economical) forms of treatment but also commit to processes that provide hope and that foster a recovery of a meaningful life.

Part of the issue here is a misapprehension that only when a person is recovered can they start to get back into society. Work, however, can be vital and useful in supporting the process of recovery itself (Warner, 2009). Presupposing that accurate diagnosis and compliance with medication are necessarily the first steps in the recovery process can themselves be barriers to recovery (Slade et al., 2014). As discussed in Chapter 3, there is emerging evidence that when it comes to using so-called antipsychotic medication, facilitating a reduction and withdrawal after initial use gives the best chance of recovery (Harrow and Jobe, 2013; Wunderink et al., 2013). Recovering a worthwhile and meaningful life is not necessarily about becoming symptom free or about not needing help from mental health or other services, although it may for some contain those things as well. Individual pathways of choice are required. Being able to participate and contribute to society is a human right and tellingly one that does not necessitate that the person change to accommodate their community until the barriers that prevent the person from participation are identified and overcome (Slade et al., 2014).

The realization here for services is that goals of personal recovery are not necessarily identical to or consistent with clinical goals of treatment; neither may goals of personal recovery be assisted by or enhanced through existing clinical processes. A radical rethink may be required for what the service and the professionals provide. For nursing in particular, it is overdue to shift meaningfully away from being a treatment-focused support towards becoming a psychological therapeutic coach, with a focus on maximizing health, striving towards desired life goals and an underlying focus of supporting social justice.

Distinguishing between recovering 'from' and being 'in recovery'

Just as the concepts of illness and health and well-being are broad and varied (or 'heterogeneous') and are not necessarily mutually dependent on each other (i.e. it is possible to experience a sense of well-being whilst having an illness), so the concept of recovery is also spectrum-like. This much is already evident from traditional outcome-based research looking at the long-term outcomes of people diagnosed with some kind of psychosis (e.g. Harding et al., 1987; see Chapter 1 of this volume). Here a useful distinction is made by Davidson and Roe (2007) between the ideas of 'recovery from' and 'recovery in' severe mental illness experiences. These are distinct but contiguous ideas that can overlap within and between people who are seeking recovery in their mental health.

We know that recovery from psychosis occurs far more frequently than perhaps is given credit for in the clinical domain: from the longitudinal studies, it seems that from 45% to 65% of people make a partial to full recovery (Davidson and Roe, 2007). This is, of course, within the limits of research methodologies, the confines of treatment regimens of the period and the ability to work with samples of participants that are sufficiently generalizable to the wider population. It is clear that recovery-from in this sense is both possible – that there is cause for hope – but also is heterogeneous – meaning that it is subject to a considerable amount of variation within the population of those identified as recovered. For the remaining proportion of the population, the second sense of recovery as in recovery-in is perhaps more pertinent.

This borrows from the independent living, self-help and addiction approaches (Davidson and Roe, 2007) wherein, even in the face of continued experience of mental health difficulties, there is a sense of recovery in *the striving pursuit* of a worthwhile and meaningful life. 'Recovery', as a term, tends to imply that something has been obtained (it has an outcome connotation), whereas this second sense – and the major thrust of personal recovery approaches – is in the support of the striving pursuit. For some, a variety of reasons and factors prevent them from taking up the striving pursuit that is being in recovery. This may be because, as an example, their experiences are too pain-laden and over-whelming and because, to some extent, acceptance of them as a form of ill health may be presently a step too far or beyond their capabilities at that moment; they are 'languishing', to borrow from Keyes' (2002) complete state model of mental health.

In these kinds of circumstances, recovery-focused mental health care in particular needs to focus on helping the person survive with as much dignity as possible, with compassionate nurturance cultivating hope by actively supporting the development of safety and comfort (Davidson and Roe, 2007). Listening Mindfully to the wishes of people for what makes life bearable is arguably a key to developing individualized approaches to those who are struggling with and perhaps languishing in extreme mental distress.

Organizational transformation: What does it take?

A project currently underway that specifically looks at the organizational challenges to implementing recovery is Implementing Recovery Through Organisational Change (ImROC), a shared venture between the Centre for Mental Health and the Mental Health Network in the UK. Shepherd and colleagues (2014), in their most recent briefing report paper, reflect on the kinds of quality indicators and outcomes that enable organizations to measure how recovery-oriented they are.

A significant task in developing recovery-oriented services is in meeting DeSilva's (2011) recommendation of a 'co-productive' service. Co-production is the truly collaborative partnership of service-user and service-provider (Shepherd et al., 2014). Examples of co-productive practices are starting to emerge, such as joint crisis planning and personal recovery planning. Joint crisis planning is an intervention that can reduce the need for admissions to hospital under the Mental Health Act and lead to the service-user feeling more in charge of their mental health problems (Henderson et al., 2004). A simple metric, then, of an aspect of co-production could therefore be an audit of the presence and quality of joint crisis planning by a mental health service.

Further, another area that indicates the presence of recovery orientation is the use of personal budgets as a supporting infrastructure to care delivery (Alakeson and Perkins, 2012). On top of this, the judicious use of Individual Placement and Support (IPS) programmes to scaffold people with severe mental health problems to gain and hold onto paid employment (Burns et al., 2009) is also a marker of pro-recovery practices. There is good-quality empirical evidence that the IPS combination of integrated vocational and clinical support, provided in close relationship to the person's desired work position, provides two to three times the rate of employment that vocational training and sheltered work schemes provide (Shepherd et al., 2014). Finding and being supported to hold onto paid employment has a positive knock-on impact on improving confidence and well-being and reducing stigma (Shepherd et al., 2014).

Whilst it is clear that recovery is supported through quality interactions between practitioners and their patients, it is also vital that the organization in which this takes place actively supports these kinds of activities. There are a variety of measures (e.g. the recovery promotion fidelity scale) that could be used by services to keep track of both the organizational commitment and areas for improvement (Burgess et al., 2011). All of these measures have particular strengths and weaknesses that are addressed in more depth in Chapter 8.

The ImROC programme set out the ten key challenges to developing recovery-oriented services, of which Shepherd and colleagues (2014) highlight four in particular as key. These are the formation of recovery colleges, developing peer support workers, shifting from professional-led risk assessment to person-centred safety planning and the usage of recovery principles in developing standards of inpatient care and safety (Shepherd et al., 2014). The quality of evidence for these components varies considerably. Peer support workers has been subject to the 'highest' standard of research evidence (the RCT), whereas person-centred safety planning is in its empirical infancy.

Current controversies: Return to work assessment – the political agenda of welfare benefits

Whilst it is empirically recognized that paid employment is, for some people with severe mental health difficulties, a vital part of recovery

(Shepherd et al., 2014), it is also a potential source of considerable distress and trauma if not appropriately timed and supported. This is very much in evidence in the current DWP (Department of Welfare and Pensions) return to work scheme mediated by the notorious Atos assessments. In 2010, the Citizens Advice Bureau (CAB) published a damning report on the Work Capability Assessment and highlighted the injustice of a system with multiple fundamental flaws, including an assessment process that does not adequately assess the capacity of the person to work, with little attention paid to the experiences of distress, pain and exhaustion, and that was insensitive to the presence of serious illnesses (CAB, 2010).

The government estimated, when this scheme was introduced, that some 39% of claimants would be found fit for work. In fact, of those assessed, from the data published in 2010 by the government when the CAB made its briefing report, 69% were being found fit. This is clearly a significantly higher figure than expected and points to the insensitivity of the assessment process. The CAB report used a combination of case study examples of insufficiencies in the system as well as rigourous statistical evidence from the DWP in making its case. Qualitative research into the impact of the work capability assessment on mental health service-users in the North East of England by Clifton and colleagues (2013) has corroborated that the cyclic experience of assessment and reassessment was found by some to clearly drive increased anxiety and distress. It is thus vitally important politically that the recovery model is not seen as a political-economical justification/leverage for such harsh and insensitive return to work programmes. With the top-down Department of Health drive for nursing to be an evidenced-based practice with efficacious and economically effective health interventions, it seems only fair that we should demand to see reciprocal evidence-based politics.

Employment, whilst a potentially liberating and therapeutic endeavour, can clearly also have toxic qualities. Part of the issue here is a 'normative assumption' of status on the part of those employing others, the employees themselves and those supporting people into work. A narrow dominant discourse on work and being an employee assumes that those who are seeking work are the source of problems when they are unable to fulfil work demands (Roets et al., 2012). Another dominant assumption is that obtaining work is in itself an end outcome that implies autonomy and therefore the cessation of mental health support (Roets et al., 2012). Roets and colleagues (2012) call for a shift away from such normative assumptions towards a social relational citizenship assumption that demands participation and joint action and the elevation of the service-users' knowledge about what they need in terms of support within the workplace as part of an ongoing collaborative negotiation.

Conclusions

Whilst recovery originated as a hopeful set of ideas from service-users and survivors of mental health services and problems, it is now a burgeoning tangible concept in the hands of policymakers, commissioners, researchers, academics and practitioners alike. As such, it is subject to the vicissitudes of collective and organizational forces. It is the potential subject of misinterpretation, and it is important that what recovery means remains in the hands of those seeking support and recovery. It is also meaningful to think of organizations and services themselves as being 'in recovery' as distinct from being a source of refined evidence-based treatments that provide 'recovery from' distinguishable categories of proscribed illnesses.

This is not a trivial reframing: it necessitates the cultivation of a whole-organization shift in practices. Explorations of what this means for organizations and how this can be relevantly meaningfully measured and tested against useful quality metrics are being conducted in the UK through recovery-focused research and pilot programmes. In a wider context, health care delivery sits within a political-governmental context that can itself hijack care transformations for its own ends. A key issue of moving towards 'co-productive ventures' and learning from the rise of user-led ventures in developing interventions, educational and clinical practices emerge as both a challenge and a safeguard for overcoming political obstacles in adopting truly recovery-oriented services.

Chapter 8

Measuring recovery

The tyranny of psychometry

An emerging theme from the previous chapters is the need to develop ways of measuring recovery. This chapter seeks to review and explore current approaches and challenges to recovery measurement. It will critically explore the literature of empirical evidence on how this is currently conceptualized.

Why measure recovery?

The development of a recovery approach in mental health services has arisen, to some extent, as a response within clinical, academic and research domains to service-user accounts of the personal experience of recovery in severe mental health difficulties (see Chapter 2). Within the organizations mentioned, the underlying organizational-culture of evidence-based practice and the requirements of the governance of health care provision demand that clinical practice be rooted in empirical evidence. In nursing for example, the professional body demands that practitioners justify their practice as 'evidence-based' (NMC, 2006). As previously argued in Chapter 2, these value-laden demands are subject to power- and political-context-related influences.

What constitutes an evidence-based practice within the professional domain of nursing is subject to a received view of what constitutes acceptable 'evidence' (Grant et al., 2010; Salkovskis, 2002). In a science-dominated professional culture, this boils down to determining that 'efficacy' exists in the statistical significance of the measurement of variables between and within identified groups subject to bias-controlled experimental trials. Commissioning services requires that there is what has been referred to, until most recently, a system of 'payment by results' (now 'payment system'), and this involves a highly contentious and complex process of clustering service-users into groups that adhere to diagnostically informed categories and the measurement of service success by aggregated service-user data using a variety of largely treatment-focused (i.e. symptomatic) outcome measures (Royal College of Psychiatrists, 2014).

What are some of these controversies? Traditional outcome measures have sprung from assumptions about the nature of clinically significant change (Jacobson and Truax, 1991). This involves certain normative assumptions about functioning – a sense that people can be seen to conform to certain standards of functioning dichotomized as either functional or dysfunctional and that measures should be looking at the extent to which interventions lead to a shift from being closer to the dysfunctional population to being closer to the functional population. A significant issue is that, for many therapeutic outcome measure domains, there is an absence of reliable 'norm' data for both functional and dysfunctional populations (Jacobson and Truax, 1991). We don't know reliably enough for any given variable what the distribution of 'functional' scores are. This makes setting cut-off points particularly difficult. That the distribution of functional or dysfunctional scores across different outcomes measures are normal distributions is also another tenuous assumption for psychosocial health data.

Further complexities arise when you consider when to take measurements. At what point before, during and after treatment is it best to measure, and how long should change be monitored after interventions? Our most robust evidence for the success of psychological therapies tends to involve relatively short durations of follow-up. We may well therefore be at risk of commissioning services (e.g. Cognitive-Behavioural Therapy for anxiety) that provide symptomatic relief in the short term but that do little in terms of preventing a return of the difficulties in the middle to long term. This leads to some thorny ethical-economical issues. For example is it appropriate to reward and pay for a service based on treatment success after the completion of therapeutic interventions, only for individuals to perhaps deteriorate within a year of treatment?

Beyond this are questions about *what* are the meaningful outcomes to be measured and how they are determined. Can numerical scales, standardized for use with all service-users, adequately capture the individual richness and meaning of experience? Lakeman (2004) argues that the use of outcome measures invites clinicians to collude with the so-called myth of objectivity in mental health and that these technological devices serve to perpetuate and legitimate the power of psychiatry and provide a distorted lens through which we are witness to recovery. In other words, psychometric measures lend a scientific credibility to such kinds of evaluative activity. There is perhaps a real danger of services investing in making what is measured (and thus responsible for determining the continuation of service funding and commissioning) the focus of service activity at the expense of what is really useful to the service-user. It is thus Burgess and colleagues' (2011) contention that measures used to evaluate service effectiveness should place what is most useful to detecting opportunities to improve service delivery in supporting that person in their individual recovery as the central preoccupation in measurement selection. It is thus vital that measures of individual and service orientation towards recovery actively and meaningfully involve the perspective of service-users in their development.

Measures of service orientation towards recovery

Williams and colleagues (2012) recently undertook a systematic review of existing measures that seek to assess how recovery focused services are. By this they mean how much a service attempts to promote personal recovery and how much the organization of the service includes practices that are believed to be pro-recovery (Williams et al., 2012). They uncovered six measures that met their inclusion criteria, excluding measures that had no psychometric credibility, those that were staff focused in orientation and other similar features that reduced their feasibility or robustness (Williams et al., 2012). They went on to evaluate the existing measures against the CHIME (Connectedness, Hope, Identity, Meaning and Empowerment) conceptual framework of recovery (Leamy et al., 2011), which provides at present the most robust empirical explicitization of the key components of recovery-promoting practices.

In reviewing existing measures against the CHIME framework, they found that the REE (Recovery Enhancing Environment) measure was the most strongly aligned. Even this measure included relatively fewer questions on the themes of hope and identity in comparison to the others. Across all the measures they reviewed, these were the two themes that were least explored by any measure, whereas empowerment as a theme was the most reliably addressed. This perhaps points to a political-organizational bias in the conceptualization of what is significant in recovery.

It seems, then, from Williams and colleagues' (2012) review that empirical measures of service orientation towards recovery need a stronger hope and identity focus. Further, there is a dearth of research work into the psychometric properties of all these recovery scales. Most were able to provide content validity by including service-users in their construction; however, the degree and scale of involvement varied widely across the scales published. At present there is no particular measure that has well defined validity or sensitivity to outcome changes. This is of particularly vital importance to the development of recovery-oriented services if it is to survive the demands of ongoing empirical research and service evaluation. It is worth noting that there is a new measure of service-users' experience of support for their recovery in the REFOCUS trial (INSPIRE) currently in development, which is now being subject to psychometric evaluation (Slade et al., 2011). Developed explicitly from the CHIME framework, INSPIRE may prove to be the first measure of service orientation that meets fundamental empirical standards of sufficient validity, robustness and sensitivity for longitudinal research into this area of recovery.

Measures of personal recovery

Burgess and colleagues (2011) undertook a systematic review of personal measures of recovery and reviewed 22 measures. They reduced the personal measures to four in terms of meeting fundamental essential psychometric properties: the RAS (Recovery Assessment Scale), IMRS (Illness Management and Recovery Scale), STORI (Stages of Recovery Instrument) and RPI (Recovery Process Inventory). Like the aforementioned service measures, none of these personal recovery measures have as of yet established sensitivity to change. They have established, to various extents, some degree of internal consistency, validity and reliability. Internal consistency refers to the degree to which the items on the scale reflect the same constructs and are verifiably yielding the same results (Burgess et al., 2011). The validity of the instrument reflects the degree to which the scale measures what it is intended to measure. Reliability is the degree to which a measure gives consistent results. Sensitivity to change is the ability of the measure to demonstrate change over time.

Comparisons of traditional clinical outcome measures with these more user-oriented measures of recovery have found little positive correlation (ranging from 0.01 to 0.24) (Slade et al., 2008), which demonstrates the significant conceptual difference between so-called personal recovery and clinical recovery, as addressed in Chapter 2. It does, however, seem vital that, for clinical use, any measures used seek to represent the personal goals of the service-user (Andresen et al., 2010). It is thus perhaps reasonable to suggest that idiosyncratic goal-attainment scaling is an approach that should be adapted (Andresen et al., 2010: see Chapter 5 on goal striving). Resnick and fellows (2004) found that, although the severity of symptoms is inversely correlated to a recovery orientation, the reduction of symptoms does not automatically lead to psychological or personal recovery. It is thus important that services do not assume that the promotion of recovery is simply about compliance with treatment and the reduction of symptoms.

There are thus perhaps two significant themes running through the assessment of personal recovery at this level: (1) that what is being measured is significant to the individual and (2) that measures of personal recovery do not merely assess the individual alone but capture the dynamic between the person and their environment (Cavelti et al., 2012). This latter critical observation leads towards developing an argument for a more concerted effort in the sociological study of mental health recovery (Watson, 2012). Watson (2012) highlights that a limitation of a quantitative approach to measuring and studying recovery is the development of a dependency on psychologically predefined variables that preclude a more nuanced understanding of the individual meanings and experiences that are associated with the process of recovery. Continuous measurement scales that are more reflective of people's actual experiences of recovery and that are not encumbered by necessarily being based in a psychological sphere are the potential benefit of using such an approach (Watson, 2012).

So what do recovery measures look like?

The Recovery Assessment Scale (RAS) (Corrigan et al., 2004) is one of the existing scales judged by Andresen and colleagues (2010) to deliver a reasonable modicum of user-focused assessment of the intrapersonal nature of recovery. It is a 41-item self-rated measure that uses a five-point scale from 'Strongly Disagree' (0) to 'Strongly Agree' (5). Example statements from the RAS can be found in Table 8.1. It has a considerable degree of empirical pedigree in that it has been shown to demonstrate a satisfactory degree of inter-rater reliability and internal consistency. Corrigan and colleagues (2004) undertook a factor analysis of the measure and found five factors: Personal Confidence and Hope, Willingness to Ask for Help, Goal and Success Orientation, Reliance on Others and Not Dominated by Symptoms. In essence these are coherent themes that run throughout the measure.

Andresen and colleagues (2010) examined the convergent validity of the RAS by comparing how well it correlated with other recovery scales [the MHRM (Mental Health Recovery Measure) and the SISR (Self-Identified Stage of Recovery measure)]. They established that the convergent validity was good, with reasonable correlations between the measures on overall scores and for sub-scores (0.70–0.89). This establishes that the measures examined demonstrate some degree of construct

Table 8.1 Example items in Recovery Assessment Scale: Identify the factor! (© Reprinted with permission from Open University Press. Corrigan et al., 2004)

Item 3: I have goals in my life that I want to reach.	Item 22: Something good will eventually happen.
Item 23: I'm the person most responsible for my own improvement.	Item 30: I know when to ask for help.
Item 39: Even when I don't believe in myself other people do.	Item 28: My symptoms interfere less and less in my life.

validity in that these scales purport to measure the same thing (recovery processes). There is further construct validity in that the RAS and other measures negatively correlate consistently with clinical measures such as the HoNOS (Health of the Nation Outcome Scores) that are measuring traditional symptom-based clinical functioning. This confirms that these measures are focused on constructs of personal growth and well-being (see Chapter 9).

To this end, whilst there is a need for further work to establish the sensitivity of such measures as promised in the ongoing REFOCUS study work in the UK (Slade et al., 2011), there is some cause for cautious optimism. These measures are seemingly accessing something other than mere symptom reduction and act as a potentially useful clinical tool for identifying what aspects of recovery processes, at any given time point of measurement, would be useful to further the person's striving towards growth and wellness (Andresen et al., 2010). Used in conjunction with clinical measures, they can potentially enrich the assessment of the person's health status. It is, however, vitally important that the measures are not used solely to drive clinical activity and that the personally valued goals of the individual are centre-stage in care planning. One particular danger, as discussed in Chapter 7, is the co-option of recovery-oriented services into a workability programme. Employment is a potentially highly valued part of creating meaning, taking responsibility and developing autonomy and self-worth, and indeed it features strongly in some recovery measures. It should not necessarily become the sole preoccupation of recovery-oriented services, however, and there does seem to be a bias in current measures towards employability.

What is the central task of recovery being measured? Towards 'narrative recovery'

If there is a central task to clinical outcome measures that capture the presence and/or severity of symptoms, it is the impact of clinical treatments (talking therapies, medication etc.) on the experience of symptoms. If individual recovery measures are capturing some construct of 'personal growth and wellness' (Andresen et al., 2010), what kind of recovery-enhancing processes might mediate this change?

Onken and colleagues (2007), in their review and analysis of the elements of recovery, highlight the process of 're-authoring' as a pivotal recovery process that facilitates change across the conceptual themes outlined by Leamy and fellows' (2011) CHIME framework. Re-authoring is a non-linear collaborative process of narrative production with one's self and with the person's network of relatives, friends and service providers (White, 1995). Re-authoring involves shifting away from a person beset by mental health difficulties and distressing emotional and psychological experiences towards a whole person facing and overcoming significant life experiences (Onken et al., 2007). This process ascribes a positive value and meaning in the experience of mental health difficulties and distress, and this is acknowledged in the meta-synthesis of psychosis previously discussed in Chapter 3. In this analysis of combined experiences of psychosis, McCarthy-Jones and colleagues (2013) identify a coherent theme of 'reforging', or rebuilding identity. This includes the notion of 'better than new' and 'gifts from psychosis', including greater compassion for others – particularly others with the shared experience of severe perceptual distress (wherein the nature of reality is significantly different from others not 'in psychosis') – and a greater sense of creativity (McCarthy-Jones et al., 2013).

A recent project that seeks to explore the value of active, creative and collaborative co-productive re-authoring–focused recovery intervention can be found in the qualitative community 'writing for recovery' project of Taylor and fellows (2014). A user-led project, 17 service-users were engaged in a community creative writing programme that engaged them in therapeutic self-reflection through creative writing skills. This project embraced a so-called Deleuzian perspective on health and sought to acknowledge that a "strand of participants' traumatic past is institutional psychiatric treatment" (Taylor et al., 2014, p. 1). From a Deleuzian stance, health and illness are recognized as contested phenomena that encompass material, experiential and contextual dimensions straddling the biological and the social (Fox, 2011).

In the Deleuzian ontology, health is reframed from being a state of the body towards an 'assemblage' of biological, psychological and cultural contextual relations that construct a body and describe its functional boundaries (Fox, 2011). Considering ill health, an adult assemblage may well be: 'disease – health professional – medicine – health technology – daily-responsibilities – mortality' (Fox, 2011). In other words, there is an individually composed assemblage of constituents that will vary from episode to episode and from person to person. Health is thus partly a capacity and desire to form new relations (Fox, 2011). Creative productive ventures, such as Taylor and colleagues' (2014) Writing for Recovery project, seek to provide a medium in which new links can be forged with others and with existing relationships in order to enhance the sense of self and to enable the person to contextualize their experience of ill health (Fox, 2011).

This is therefore an endeavour that seeks to revise our understandings of recovery that currently are subject to the powerful distorting lenses of clinical and researcher professional practice (Taylor et al., 2014). Recovery instead is seen as an ability to "transcend invalidating social processes, which often include social discrimination and frequently the day-to-day practices of institutional psychiatry" (Taylor et al., 2014, p. 2).

Re-authoring embraces the possibilities of people using storytelling about their experiences as an approach to seek meanings that enable better coping with their past, current and future circumstances (Taylor et al., 2014). The role of the professional in co-production, then, in partnership with users, is to create opportunities to develop the skills needed for re-authoring, or 'narrative recovery'. It is perhaps pertinent to differentiate the ideas of recovery currently espoused as clinical and personal to incorporate this strand of narrative recovery. Taking experiences of suffering, mistreatment and distress and turning them into stories of survival and growth enable people to build both individual and communal resilience against stigmatizing societal actions (Taylor et al., 2014). This is validated in the themes emerging from collective qualitative research into the experience of psychosis as outlined in Chapter 3 (McCarthy-Jones et al., 2013).

It seems clear that embracing these new kinds of processes involves a recognition that there is a need for a significant shift in professional function. This shift necessitates that there is organizational support for such wider and previously unrecognized forms of activity, embracing service-users as co-producers in service development and thinking sensitively about where to locate these activities so that the environment is fit for purpose. Would the Writing for Recovery project, as described by Taylor and fellows (2014), not lose its attractiveness and power if it were contained contextually within the provision of mental health care – in, say, a hospital setting? Being willing to meet and engage participants in neutral territories or territories that maximize comfort for the participant seems a vital component for consideration. It seems disingenuous and incongruent to me that many recovery college projects that I have identified through Internet scoping searches are readily identifiable as part of the pre-existing mental health service providers rather than located within a more tangible educational setting.

Conclusions

Mental health care exists within an established dominant cultural framework that propagates (amongst many other things) values of evidence-based practice. It is regulated, monitored and provisioned through systems of quality assurance, targets and outcomes. In adopting and implementing a recovery-oriented care approach, it is thus understandable that the health care milieu seeks to establish measures that enable them to demonstrate that it is meeting regulatory and outcome-driven top-down demands. Some critics, such as Lakeman (2004), have raised the objection that mental health organizations, in doing so, are perpetuating the technical legitimacy of psychiatry. The current development of empirical measures has made progress in developing individual measures of recovery and organizational measures of recovery orientation.

It is clear that many of these measures are proving empirically rigorous and valid in terms of what they are measuring and their reliability. At present, there is a pressing need for testing the sensitivity of such measures in capturing changes in these constructs. Looking at what existing relatively empirically robust measures of recovery actually measure highlights the importance of the intrapersonal. Given that recovery has a well-being and growth focus, we looked at the role of re-authoring as a significant process construct. I proposed a further differentiation of recovery to include narrative recovery and highlighted some of the potential shifts that mental health professionals will need to engage with and to facilitate relevant interventions.

Chapter 9

Beyond recovery

Towards mental health as well-being

This chapter explores the issues of psychological well-being as an area that mental health services need to address in developing recovery-oriented services. This is defined, and relevant related concepts are addressed. A critical review of evidence-based interventions that seek to improve well-being is provided. Once again, relevant empirical evidence and theory will be articulated and critiqued, as well as relevant post-modernist considerations.

Why should recovery-oriented services address well-being?

An emerging parallel strand of psychological research that sits alongside but that developed independently from current recovery research is that of positive psychology. Because the user-instigated recovery movement emerged from grass roots (typically American grass roots), survivor accounts called for, amongst other things, the development of services sensitive to the 'consumer voice'. In parallel, a shift into the development of 'positive psychology', grounded in empiricism, arose within the field of psychology itself (Resnick and Rosenheck, 2006). Positive psychology seeks to develop a body of knowledge grounded in the empirical study of how to empower people to enhance what is already good and helpful, fostering positive emotions and creating a life predicated on meaningful experiences (Resnick and Rosenheck, 2006). An approach that has shown some successful traction, for those who do not labour under the added burden of diagnosed mental health difficulties, is the incorporation of a 'strengths focus' into the person's life (Resnick and Rosenheck, 2006).

There seem to be clear parallels and synergistic advantages here for drawing upon the developing empirical evidence afforded by the positive psychology intellectual and academic movement and the rising recovery movement that is in itself clamouring for empirical validation.

Health and illness: Not even the same coin!

It is perhaps the de facto position by virtue of psychiatry that mental health is at one end of a single bipolar dimension that is opposed by mental illness (Keyes, 2005, 2006). This largely untested assumption has perhaps persisted for as long as it has because of the robust evidence that those who labour under difficulties like 'depression' are less productive and satisfied with their lives than those who are not (Daig et al., 2009). It is also folly to dispute the fact that mental health difficulties are a significant world-wide public health concern. It is also hardly surprising that the initial and continuing (to some extent) preoccupation with the ironically titled 'mental health' services across the world is in dealing with the morbidity and ameliorating the mortality associated with 'mental illness'. 'Mental health' (or well-being/flourishing) as such barely gets a look-in.

Looking closely at the question of how mental health and mental illness interrelate, however, chips heavily away at this often unquestioned axiom. It is an assumption that people who are free of mental health difficulties necessarily feel or function well (Keyes, 2005, 2006). It is also emerging from a variety of bodies of evidence that positive and negative affects constitute two correlated factors (see e.g. Tellegen et al., 1999). In other words, an individual may not necessarily feel sad, but that does not necessarily mean that they will thus experience high levels of happiness.

Naïve assumptions about the constituent structures and relationships that intra-psychically make up our mental lives are exactly that – naïve assumptions that break down under the lens of empirical scrutiny. It is thus vital for clinicians, academics, educators and researchers to view mental illness and mental health as potentially coexistent experiential properties, in which mental health is something positive and more than the absence of illness. This is encouraging from a theoretical perspective and suggests that treatments combining approache to reduce the impact of distress and mental ill health, alongside approaches for improving mental health or well-being, should prove efficacious. They would also align services more coherently with the World Health Organisation's (WHO) declaration that health is "[a] state of complete physical, mental and social well-being and not merely the absences of disease or infirmity" (WHO, 1946, p. 100).

According to Layard (2005), drawing from a large survey of the American population, the top seven factors contributing to longer-term happiness are family relationships, financial situation, work, community and friends, health, personal freedom and personal values. Huppert (2009) construes a life worth living as involving not only the pursuit of happiness but also the capacity to be resilient in the face of adversity. It is perhaps controversial theoretically to incorporate resilience as such an integral part of mental health, but it could also be argued that being unable to cope with and withstand emotional stressors is a barrier to experiencing your life as worthwhile and euthymogenic (happiness generating).

Empirical evidence for positive psychological interventions (PPI)

Bolier and colleagues (2013) undertook a systematic review and meta-analysis of randomized controlled trials of positive psychology interventions. They reviewed 39 studies representing some 6,139 participants. These interventions included self-help interventions, group sessions and individualized positive psychological therapy. Overall, the meta-analysis concluded that positive psychology interventions produced a small but significant treatment efficacy on measures of subjective well-being (0.34), psychological well-being (0.20) and depression (0.23). This is a fairly significant and rapid achievement given that the first serious research studies of positive psychology interventions began only a little over a decade ago, following Seligman and Csikszentmihalyi's (2000) pioneering seminal article critiquing the negative bias of psychology and calling for a 'positive psychology' approach.

The approaches that have demonstrable efficacy include – 'counting your blessings', 'practicing kindness', 'setting personal goals', 'expressing gratitude' and using 'personal strengths' (Bolier et al., 2013). Of these interventions, their meta-analysis found that higher effect sizes were found for interventions of a longer duration and that were individualized (compared to self-help) (Bolier et al., 2013). The personalization of interventions to the person's needs and face-to-face support seem to be factors that moderate and improve the efficacy of self-help positive psychology interventions (Bolier et al., 2013).

An example of synthesizing positive psychology interventions with problem-based psychotherapeutic approaches: Padesky and Mooney's strengths-based CBT

An example of integrating principles of positive psychology interventions as an additional strand of existing psychotherapeutic work can be found in Padesky and Mooney's (2012) Four-Step Strengths-Based CBT (Cognitive-Behavioural Therapy) approach. This model of CBT encourages clinicians to help clients actively seek out their valued strengths. This involves the clinician listening out for potential strengths that are 'hidden' in or obscured by a problem-saturated story. For instance, from a strengths perspective, consider the story of a single mother, on benefits, who seeks help from mental health services because of considerable distress that one of her three children is struggling with her performance at school. She is dreadfully worried that social services may take away her child.

Putting on our strengths-focused spectacles, we can start to see that there are possible hidden strengths here. This is a woman who single-handedly is managing to keep all three of her children in school. She is living on benefits and presumably must have some considerable budgeting skills to run her household – again, single-handedly. Her other children are presumably doing well enough at school not to be a concern. Somehow she is able to organize and manage her day so that all three attend school. There are some testable assumptions here, in dialogue with the person to explore things that she is doing well, and indeed resiliently by overcoming perhaps daily challenges and obstacles.

We already know that counting-your-blessings is an intervention in the PPI arsenal that can improve subjective and psychological well-being. Helping the mother to acknowledge the areas of her life that are going well through gentle guided discovery could help her to become less critical of herself and thus have some knock-on benefit in terms of her mood and self-esteem, if these prove to be relevant issues. In Padesky and Mooney's (2012) model, the clinician would help the client actively identify her strengths in areas outside the problem domain. The process then moves on to explore whether any of these strengths involve strategies that have been tested by life obstacles and to explore how these difficulties had been surmounted: that is what are the resilient strategies? In doing so, the aim is to build a personal model of resilience (PMR) (Padesky and Mooney, 2012).

Having developed an individualized model of strategies that the person already has, with a proven track record in other life areas, the person in therapy and the clinician work together to see whether strategies from their PMR might be adapted and applied to areas of their life that are identified as problematic. Homework is set collaboratively to look out for opportunities in the problem domain in order to apply these strategies with the objective of being resilient rather than necessarily immediately resolving the issue. This tack can help the person to avoid some degree of reactive distress, or 'collapse', in the face of stress, and it can be combined with coping techniques and other CBT strategies (e.g. testing out how useful and valid negative thoughts and predictions are about self and others) in order to formulate new, more helpful ways of making sense of things.

As a side note, it's worth noting that Padesky and colleagues (2011) have constructed one of the first measures in Cognitive-Behavioural Therapy that seeks to evaluate therapist conceptualization competence as well as measuring the strength and resilience focus of sessional work. The Collaborative Case Conceptualization Rating Scale (CCCRS) is thus one of the few existing measures that operationalizes a model of formulation and measures therapist fidelity to this model (Padesky et al., 2011). The central principles of this model are that the 'level' of case formulation best fits the stage of therapy and is no more complex than it needs be (a principle of parsimony), that therapy is a collaborative process grounded in empirical research and that equal attention is paid to the strengths and resilience of the person (Padesky et al., 2011).

Recovery and well-being

Some leading researchers in the field of recovery, such as Slade (2010), have argued that mental health services will need to embrace new approaches in order to move the focus to promoting people's well-being, as well as working to effectively treat their 'mental illness'. Slade (2010) goes on to argue that, since a common theme that repeats itself in recovery narratives is the person engaging in their life and in part this is due to finding meaning and a sense of fruitful purpose, this directs mental health services clearly towards the need for working to improve well-being. If recovery is aligned as goal striving towards better mental health even in the presence of mental illness, then a recurring critical objection can be readily countered. This is the often raised objection: how can you be 'recovered' if you still experience symptoms of mental illness? An issue here, as Slade (2009) surmises, is that 'recovery' is a term that is laden with connotations of illness. As such, it perhaps serves to lead people to fall unwittingly into the untested single bipolar mental health/illness continuum trap without appreciating the multidimensionality of these psychological constructs. The answer to the objection is of course that health and illness are not simply polar opposites.

Resistance to well-being

A shift in focus to well-being has not been without some resistance and critical response. Some psychologists and researchers are unclear as to whether interventions that focus on 'well-being exercises' will be sufficient to prevent the need for psychiatric intervention (Carlisle and Hanlon, 2008). Eckersley (2006) points out that, in the rush to produce a science of well-being, we may be at risk of confounding statistical correlations for causations. For example, measures of well-being often tend to focus on happiness. Happiness can be linked to a degree of 'self-deception' – that is an exaggerated sense of optimism and over-confidence in the ability to control and shape life. This is indeed borne out in some recent American studies that highlight the potential dangers of being excessively optimistic – namely a risk of becoming unrealistically positive and blinded to potential dangers in life (Lillienfeld and Arkowitz, 2011). Another critical point is that happiness is an inherently subjective experience. We must therefore be wary of evidence derived from survey data that can also be vulnerable to the assumptions of those undertaking the research.

Where is social well-being? Towards digital communities

So far the psychological approach to well-being has tended to focus on personal functioning in its examination of the phenomenon. Whilst there is no doubt that well-being has a 'private' face, there is also the distinction of the 'public' life to be considered (Keyes, 1998). As individuals, we are embedded, to varying degrees, in social contexts and communities. It thus makes sense to consider how the social nature of life and the challenges it contains may constitute criteria that people use in assessing their lives (Keyes, 1998). Social well-being, then, is perhaps "the appraisal of one's circumstance and functioning in society" (Keyes, 1998, p. 122). Recognizing this, Keyes (1998) developed a measure of social well-being that focuses on five factors: social actualization, social acceptance, social integration, social contribution and social coherence.

Of those five factors, social actualization is the person's belief in and hopefulness about the condition and future of society. It is a measure of the sense that society is in charge of its future and destiny. Social coherence is the perception of the quality, constitution and functioning of the social world – in other words, that society is predictable and sensible. Social integration is the assessment of the quality of the individual's relationship to society and community. Another way of putting it is the feeling that you have something in common with others in your social network. Social acceptance is the degree to which the person feels able to trust others and thinks that others in their community are kind and helpful – in other words, the degree to which you find that your social context is favourable and accepting. Finally, social contribution is an assessment or measure of the person's social value: that is how vital are you to your social community?

It is perhaps hardly surprising that there should be overlaps between these ideas that are elsewhere referred to as 'social capital' and 'subjective well-being'. Acknowledging the social context of the delivery of mental health care is perhaps something that is overlooked in everyday clinical practice. What are the potential benefits from attending to the more sociological aspects of well-being? Well, for example knowing that social connectedness in its many forms has a uniformly positive effect on people's physical health and that ratings of physical health are also a component of subjective well-being (Helliwell and Putnam, 2004) strongly suggests that, in working with people to improve their mental health and well-being, facilitating social networking is a worthwhile structural social intervention. This may include supporting the person to access social communities by using technologically assisted forms of social networking. It would seem to make sense, then, that people, in distress and potentially isolated from others for example whilst on mental health wards, should be able to maintain and build connections with others through technological social networking. Very little formal research has been committed to date in studying the crossovers between developing forms of social communication and its effects on mental health, and there is considerable variation in clinical practice.

Professional bodies are only just coming to grips with the presence of their health and social care professionals on networks such as Twitter and Facebook, and issues of confidentiality and professional conduct tend to be of primary concern (NMC, 2010). The rise of 'digital' mental health through the use of technologically supported media (e.g. blogging, micro blogging, forums, chat rooms) that scaffold connectedness and possibly extend into virtual communities is an area that mental health practitioners should invest interest and participate in. It is a new frontier of mental health practice – a new place in which we can meet with people in need of professional support with regard to their mental health. Indeed, some of the social media places are rather wild and unkempt – but they are simultaneously open to new developments and innovative practices to evolve into.

Another area in which the properties of social media provide a particular advantage is in the representation of identity. With recovery-oriented practice, there is a conceptual shift away from identifying with 'illness' as the main domain that mental health difficulties impact towards the effect it has on identity (as discussed at some length in Chapter 5). In creating a presence on Twitter, people have the freedom of a number of options: they may choose to acknowledge and identify with their mental health difficulties and diagnosis and retain a personal anonymity within that. Alternatively, others choose to link themselves to their mental health identity. Others still prefer to dis-identify from this.

So there is a sense that, given an opportunity to create a representation of self, the person can choose how explicitly and transparently to acknowledge their relationship to their mental health experiences. For some users of Twitter, there are certain kudos and status afforded by this explicit representational link to their lived experience, as is evident in the rise of 'experts by experience' (Scourfield, 2009). In social media, people are able to contribute a critical voice across dialogues, where it is down to individual users choosing whom to follow and what conversational threads to participate in. People are readily accessible. People with lived experience are increasingly bringing their experiential expertise to awareness-raising campaigns, blogs and dialogue with professionals, researchers and educationalists on how we talk about, understand and work with our mental health. Whereas professionals are to some extent or other bound to follow certain constraints on how they conduct themselves in the shared social space (this varies according to the regulatory development of the respective professional bodies), this constraint does not necessarily act upon other groups. There is a sort of 'hierarchical flattening' in this dialogical space, although this does not mean that there are not status-focused disagreements, conflicts and controversies in interactions between service-users and 'professionals'.

Conclusions

Recovery and well-being are two closely related concepts. In the context of health and illness, it's important to acknowledge that there is a clear multidimensionality to these constructs. Recovery, as it is in the current UK context, is as much a social justice movement that has made an impact on the development of practice and mental health policy. It is now starting to accrue some empirical evidence, which in some respects amounts to becoming inculcated into the dominant master narrative of evidenced-based practice that holds sway in medical and nursing practice. Positive psychology, in contrast, has a stronger empirical basis and amounts to a significant critical challenge to the established orthodox paradigm of prior psychological research. Recovery-oriented practice has the opportunity to shape its strands of clinical practice by borrowing from the developing evidence of positive psychology.

Given the barriers inherent in 'recovery' as a term – particularly its unfortunate illness and medical connotations – it might make more sense to talk in a Keyesian sense about 'growth and well-being' as an alternative. Some of the existing positive psychology strategies include strengths-focused work and strategies to develop resilience. An example of a synthesis of more traditionally problem-focused psychotherapy with positive psychological strategies was Padesky and Mooney's (2012) Four-Step Strengths-Based CBT approach.

A shortcoming of current well-being–focused work is the very research that it is predicated upon – significantly from questionnaire-based survey approaches. More rigourous controlled trials are needed, particularly for people with significant emotional and psychological health difficulties, in order for PPI to rise to the empirically based recovery challenge and not fall short of being insufficient to ward off the psychiatrist, as commenters have predicted.

Finally, the virtues of considering the wider social context of the delivery of care and the role of social factors in contributing to the experience and attainment of well-being were addressed. An exciting possibility of finding new ways to meaningfully engage with people with mental health and recovery needs lies in the use of technologically supported social media. Specific research into the impact that the usage of social media has on identity and recovery is an objective that nursing research would do well to develop.

Chapter 10

Reflections upon recovery

The person is political

This chapter attempts to synthesize the main themes and issues relating to the empirical evidence on recovery and the relevant critical aspects of its relationship to lived experience. It forms a critically reflective essay and includes autoethnographic reflections of my own experience of psychosis and recovery.

Recovery as a catalyst for change

Recovery has arisen as a clarion call from survivors of mental health difficulties and treatment services – a call to challenge the overly pessimistic portrayal of psychosis as a necessarily chronic condition. This undue pessimism continues to the present day. In her Technology, Entertainment and Design (TED) talk on hearing voices, Eleanor Longden talked about how it felt when her psychiatrist told her that she'd have been better off with a diagnosis of cancer than schizophrenia because cancer can be treated and cured (Longden, 2013). On top of this, the ideas of 'recovery', as originally espoused, intended to demonstrate that there is hope for living a meaningful and fulfilling life despite the stigma and potentially life-threatening arrival of 'severe mental illness'. For others, recovery is thus also about galvanizing social justice activities and challenging the status-quo of psychiatry-as-was and mostly psychiatry-as-is. It is borne out of the voices of 'the other' to draw from the language of Dussellian trans-modernism (see Chapter 2).

Recovery, however, has since become part of the professional arena, particularly as researchers into mental health and psychiatry have sought to clarify what is meant by 'personal recovery'. Scientific approaches are at work to identify its constituents and processes. In doing so, recovery has become vulnerable to being lost in translation or distorted as it filters into organizational practice. In light of this possibility, it is in some sense heartening that initial programmes evaluating the implementation of a recovery-oriented focus have sought to find ways of measuring not only the individual's personal recovery but also the organization's adherence to recovery principles.

There remains, however, the considerable threat that, politically, recovery becomes a means of higher-order justification for leveraging against people in need of ongoing support and help from the welfare benefits system. Recovery as an ethos has been enthusiastically received within research and academia but perhaps less well received and understood within day-to-day clinical practice. The professional version of recovery, by virtue of being transplanted as a story of survival and an account of deliverance from the hands of institutional treatment, is also in danger of being perceived as and indeed being transformed into a significantly different animal in the hands of health care organizations. It's thus important to foster partnerships with service-users/survivors that extends well beyond tokenistic inclusion and to be open to critique and change within the recovery movement. It is also important to consider that mental health organizations themselves are in need of 'recovery'.

EXPERIENCING RECOVERY: VALUING STORYTELLING

My own recovery from psychosis did not really begin significantly until I had successfully disentangled myself from acute and then community mental health services. That's not to say that I don't think I couldn't have benefited from professional support at this time; it is just that, at the time of my experience of mental distress and the state of services, freeing myself from the identity of mental patient was a much needed step. I don't think this was really a specific goal for me at this time: that is it wasn't a conscious decision. However, I was aware that, all the time I was being 'supported' by community services, the prospect of re-entering the workplace or undertaking some kind of meaningful study as means of becoming a productive person was held in abeyance. For me, a satisfying life is predominantly the 'meaningful life' – that is one with purpose. I sought to leave services at the time because I didn't see them as doing anything useful for me, and indeed they were a lumbering obstacle to my getting on with life.

Part of this process for me involved getting out of the mental health ghetto of supported housing and day-hospital services. Having an outside community of other mental health service-users – all to some degree or other struggling to manage their own individual personal and social integrity – was a part of this. Until I'd managed to find a source of paid employment that could springboard me out of the benefits system, I had to find ways of connecting with others that wasn't a financial drain. Once every two weeks when my benefits came in, I treated myself to fried chicken and chips. Then it was back to beans on toast and pasta for the remainder of the fortnight. I thus found community in free workshops run by churches and voluntary organizations. I got back into employment by working for the Samaritans for a period, although I always felt that employees who worked for nothing were held in tacit contemptuous disregard. I went to juggling workshops and made efforts to socialize with people who were not under the umbrella of services. I still had friends from 'the system' and spent time with them but found this hard to maintain because it meant having contact with mental health services.

I tried and failed over a period of time to reclaim some sense of integrity and identity by getting involved in activities. I ran a martial arts class in a community centre one day a week for a while and applied for an arts diploma course at the local college. Neither of these activities bore much fruit, but I realize retrospectively that I was seeking a means of promoting my identity as something other than a person with mental illness. I was also looking for a sense of security and meaningfulness in my day-to-day self, having spent years not being able to rely or trust on the validity of my experience. It thus seems to me to be particularly vital to shift the place where the professional meets the service-user and that the person is met with hope for change. It's also essential that the person's individual preferences and values are understood and central to any care plans – crucial in terms of getting 'employment' right. Yes, the Samaritans voluntary work (instigated by my care coordinator) helped me get back into a routine, but it didn't fit with my vision for how I wanted my life to be.

Reflecting on current treatments for psychosis

The mainstay of current UK treatments remains antipsychotic medication, alongside anxiolytics, antidepressants and mood-stabilizing medicines. There is no doubt that antipsychotics specifically can have a powerful effect and that the distressing experiences of unusual beliefs and thoughts, voices and seeing things that others cannot can be changed through the use of such medications. It is also clear that in the longer term, these medicines have potentially very harmful unwanted effects and that even full compliance with the prescribing regime may still subject a person to difficult experiences. There is now some emerging evidence that long-term sustained use of antipsychotic medications across the board means that some people who would be able to recover are prevented from doing so. A shift towards tapering after two or three years of initial treatment and working with the person to support trials of reducing medication should become a more mainstream approach.

EXPERIENCING ANTIPSYCHOTIC MEDICATION

A critique that I have some affinity for is that these medications are not specifically antipsychotic (Moncrieff, 2009). There is no doubt that they have that property, but it has a rather sledgehammer effect on overall conscious experience. I found my mental acuity (or sense of fluidity and sharpness of thinking) to be considerably dulled on these medications. I also found, as time wore on, that it was more difficult to feel. To my consultant, this was evidence of 'negative symptoms'. That I was (from my perspective) prone to periods of depression and also found that my emotional experience seemed to be altered by the medication were continuously rejected as possibilities. It would have been a particularly sad day when I found I couldn't enjoy listening to my favourite music, were I able to connect with that emotion! It was a peculiarly detached experience. Similarly, I recall the delight when this experience returned after getting off the drugs; it was in fact sadness at hearing one of my favourite rather soulful tunes that generated such delight. Feeling any emotions – positive or negative – I found much more preferable to being what seemed to be permanently divorced from them.

Psychological treatments

I can't comment meaningfully on the experience of receiving psychological treatments during my experience and recovery from psychosis. I never had any in that respect. I rarely had any meaningful one-to-one discussion with health care professionals that didn't consist of my answering a million-and-one questions that largely seemed to focus on how at risk I felt.

When I entered into mental health practice from the opposite end, as a qualified nurse, I was determined to bring an aspect of talking therapeutic care into my practice. My experience of using Cognitive-Behavioural Therapies for people with psychosis is that it can make a meaningful impact upon the psychological experience of the person. This is based on what they've told me and how they have been able to get on with the business of living, having gotten beyond surviving their experience. This is rather lost in the current empirical evaluations of research efficacy. In the clamour of science to develop methods that control for intrinsic bias towards valuing the statistical significance of differences in averaged populations on objectively assessed scales, the person's experience has rather fallen to the wayside. It has become invalidated in the process of science.

Something about the recovery ethos has stimulated a resurgence in valuing the person's experience. Working with someone in a clinical setting is necessarily an individually oriented experience. That is not to say that the wider context is ignored or that relevant others should not be included in the planning, delivery and evaluation of care. However, what works for the person and the impact that interventions have on them are best judged by that individual for it's their experience that interventions are aimed at. It is thus on some level a paradox that we are overseen in our evidence-based practice by an approach that does little to embrace the rich diversity of a person's experience and indeed denies the value of individual subjectivity. I would thus endorse calls to embrace ethnography as a source of understanding the nature of experience and the development of mixed-method approaches to humanize the quantitative.

Recovery research and measuring recovery

On one hand, I think there is just cause to be cautious about the application of research to recovery. At the same time, whilst there is the appreciable risk of the hopeful ideas becoming hijacked and sanitized as they are absorbed into the dominant discourse of mental health care services, there is also the possibility that it will spark the transformation of services and thinking into less coercive, more person-centred systems of care.

I have subtitled this chapter as 'The Person Is Political'. This phrase, or rather the phrase 'The Personal Is Political', was coined by the feminist writer Carol Hanisch in 1969 in her thus titled paper (Hanisch, 1970). I have adapted it slightly and am using it because, to me, recovery in mental health services embodies some of the central arguments Hanisch was making in talking about women's liberation – except here we are talking about liberation for people with 'significant mental health difficulties'. The best judges of course as to whether these difficulties are 'significant' are the persons themselves, but often it comes down to outsiders and relative strangers making decisions about the person's life in the context of an organization's hard-pressed and skewed resources. The person is thus political. They are 'users' of services, a potential drain on resources, and they are a risk to themselves and others that must be safeguarded. Lots of things are deemed necessary to 'do unto them' and to take away from them. They almost become depersonalized objects within the system of care. Statistics counted and categorized with tracked outcomes are used to justify the existence and funding of the service working with them.

These are all potentially highly dehumanizing and indeed degrading experiences, and it is a significant risk on the part of the person to trust professional services. It is hard to calculate how many people opt out of services as part of their self-care because they find services not only unhelpful but ultimately restrictive and damaging.

I am thus encouraged by the focus on inductive qualitative research as a foundation of recovery research. The CHIME conceptual framework for example, from which a measure of organizational fidelity to recovery-oriented practice has been constructed (INSPIRE), seems to me to be a high-quality example of where empirical research can 'listen to' and learn from the collected experiences of people in services. That's not to say there aren't threats within this. Qualitative research is at much at risk from bias as its quantitative and significantly more well regarded sibling. The meta-synthesis approach to constructing a body of knowledge on psychosis is, on the face of it, yet again an inductive approach grounded in the experiences of people who have encountered psychosis. It is laudable for this reason but again subject to bias in that those who conduct the research inevitably will introduce an element of 'spin' and selectivity in how they present and represent their data. We must therefore be cautious that in applying such knowledge, we should not take for granted the persons sitting before us and expect them to fit into this 'model' or 'framework'. Instead, we should be at pains to adapt the 'model' or 'framework' to them. Perhaps it is better to think of this kind of research as, more than anything else, formulating guiding principles for clinical work. It's also vital that, when organizations and services are making use of fidelity measures, these measures don't themselves become the focus of the organization's activities. The service isn't there to improve how well it measures on some scale or checklist per se.

'Identity vs. illness'

A significant thematic change in this alleged paradigmatic shift in mental health (from traditional psychiatry to recovery-based psychiatry) seems to me to be reflected in moving away from viewing people as being attached to illnesses. If we have this view front and centre, then the purpose of services is to work with the illness. Identify it . . . delineate it . . . diagnose it and, from this, prescribe evidence-based treatments that work upon the illness itself. When this is the case, the person rather gets lost in the clamour for accurate assessment, diagnosis, treatments, treatment reviews and so forth. If we place the identity of the person front and centre, we get the opportunity to work with them from a radically different perspective. It forces us to ask questions about how we talk to the person. Is what we are doing as professionals getting in the way of that person's exploration of self and self-development? Are we working according to their desires and goals or according to our treatment guidelines and the dictates of evidence-based practice? These are potent questions in the hands of reflexive practitioners.

'Illness and recovery' vs. 'growth and well-being'

A parallel shift comes from working with a person to grow from experiences – not necessarily to cure them of the harmful aspects of experiences because that somehow entails a sort of censorship, as if some part of experience ought to be somehow deleted or eradicated. Instead, perhaps it is more germane to develop a position of fostering psychological and emotional flexibility, embracing contextualized therapeutic approaches as currently best personified by Acceptance- and Mindfulness-based approaches. Looking towards interventions that can support the social infrastructure of experience to enhance social well-being, as well as this individual's psychological well-being. This is not a trivial shift, and it does not mean abandoning current treatment practices and work on the prevention of abuse. It is a widening of purpose for mental health practitioners and legitimizes social justice activities, lobbying for political change when there is an injustice that is systemically exacerbating suffering.

It also calls for developing a co-productive philosophy in the development, implementation and evaluation of services and care. Service-user 'inclusion' is the predominant trend but is again subject to being tokenistic and serving only to maintain the status quo. Who decides which service-users get to be 'included', and what do they get to be 'included' in? These political dimensions of recovery are inescapable. They can, however, be critiqued and challenged in situ. It should be ethically incumbent upon us, as mental health professionals, to challenge such political chicaneries and work to change them from within organizations. Sometimes this will require us to forsake ownership of things that are better off in the hands of the 'other' to facilitate change. Recovery provides us with an opportunity to reform systems of mental health care by effecting change within our practices. As practitioners, we would do well to grasp the fundamentals of recovery-oriented practice and place ourselves as practitioners into recovery with regard to our clinical practices.

Bibliography

Abba, N., Chadwick, P., and Stevenson, C. (2008). **Responding mindfully to distressing psychosis: A grounded theory analysis**. Psychotherapy Research, 18, 77–87.

Aghotor, J., Pfueller, U., Moritz, S., Weisbrod, M., and Roesch-Ely, D. (2010). **Meta-cognitive training for patients with schizophrenia: Feasibility and preliminary evidence for its efficacy**. Journal of Behavioural Therapy and Experimental Psychiatry, 41, 207–211.

Alakeson, V., and Perkins, R. (2012). **Recovery, personalisation and personal budgets**. London: Centre for Mental Health.

American Psychiatric Association. (1987). **Diagnostic and statistical manual of mental disorders (3rd edition, revised) (DSM-III-R)**. Washington, DC: Author.

Andersson, G., Asmundson, G.J., Carlbring, P., Ghaderi, A., Hofmann, S.G., and Stewart, S.H. (2005). **Is CBT already the dominant paradigm in psychotherapy research and practice?** Cognitive Behaviour Therapy, 34 (1), 1–2.

Andresen, R., Caputi, P., and Oades, L.G. (2010). **Do clinical outcome measures assess consumer-defined recovery?** Psychiatry Research, 177 (3), 309–317.

Andresen, R., Oades, L., and Caputi, P. (2003). **The experience of recovery from schizophrenia: Towards an empirically validated stage model**. Australian and New Zealand Journal of Psychiatry, 37, 586–594.

Anthony, W.A. (1993). **Recovery from mental illness: The guiding vision of the mental health service system in the 1990's**. Psychosocial Rehabilitation Journal, 16 (4), 11–23.

Bach, P., and Hayes, S.C. (2002). **The use of acceptance and commitment therapy to prevent the rehospitalisation of psychotic patients: A randomised controlled trial**. Journal of Consulting Clinical Psychology, 70, 1129–1139.

Bakhtin, M.M. (1981). **The dialogic imagination: Four essays**. Edited by M. Holquist. Austin: University of Texas Press.

Barch, D.M. (2005). **The cognitive neuroscience of schizophrenia**. Annual Review of Clinical Psychology, 1, 321–353.

Barrowclough, C., Tarrier, N., Humphreys, L., Ward, J., Gregg, L., and Andrews, B. (2003). **Self-esteem in schizophrenia: Relationships between** self-evaluation, family attitudes and symptomology. Journal of Abnormal Psychology, 112 (1), 92–99.

Bassett, J., Lloyd, C., and Bassett, H. (2001). Work issues for young people with psychosis: Barriers to employment. British Journal of Occupational Therapy, 64, 66–72.

Bentall, R.P., Kinderman, P., and Kaney, S. (1994). The self, attributional processes and abnormal beliefs: Towards a model of persecutory delusions. Behaviour Research and Therapy, 32, 331–341.

Beresford, P. (2012). Presentation in Recovery 2012 Conference. [Online] http://vimeo.com/41967871 [Accessed: 07/01/2014].

Berger, P.L., and Luckmann, T. (1966). The social construction of reality: A treatise in the sociology of knowledge. New York: Anchor Books.

Berrios, G.E., and Hodges, J.R. (eds.). (2000). Memory disorders in psychiatric practice. Cambridge: Cambridge University Press.

Bieling, P.J., and Kuyken, W. (2003). Is cognitive case formulation science or science fiction? Clinical Psychology: Science and Practice, 10 (1), 52–69.

Birchwood, M., Mason, R., and MacMillan, F. (1993). Depression, demoralization and control over psychotic illness: A comparison of depressed and non-depressed patients with a chronic psychosis. Psychological Medicine, 23, 387–395.

Birchwood, M., and Trower, P. (2006). The future of cognitive-behavioural therapy for psychosis: Not a quasi-neuroleptic. British Journal of Psychiatry, 188, 107–108.

Bird, V., Leamy, M., Le Boutillier, C., Williams, J., and Slade, M. (2011). REFOCUS: Promoting recovery in community mental health services. London: Rethink.

Bogár, K., and Perczel, D.F. (2007). Trauma and psychosis. Psychiatry Hungary, 22 (4), 300–310.

Bolier, L., Haverman, M., Westerhof, G.J., Riper, H., Smit, F., and Bohlmeijer, E. (2013). Positive psychology interventions: A meta-analysis of randomized controlled studies. BMC Public Health, 13, 1–20.

Bond, G.R., Resnick, S.G., Drake, R.E., Xie, H., McHugo, G.J., and Bebout, R.R. (2001). Does competitive employment improve nonvocational outcomes for people with severe mental illness? Journal of Consulting and Clinical Psychology, 69, 489–501.

Bonney, S., and Stickley, T. (2008). Recovery and mental health: A review of the British literature. Journal of Psychiatric and Mental Health Nursing, 15, 140–153.

Bracken, P., and Thomas, P. (2001). Postpsychiatry: A new direction for mental health. British Medical Journal, 322, 724.

Brooks, D. (2012). The social animal: The hidden sources of love, character, and achievement. New York: Random House.

Broome, M.R., Johns, L.C., Valli, I., Woolley, J.B., Tabraham, P., Brett, C., Valmaggia, L., Peters, E., Garety, P.A., and McGuire, P.K. (2007). Delusion formation and reasoning biases in those at clinical high risk for psychosis. British Journal of Psychiatry, 191, 38–42.

Bruner, J.S. (1986). **Actual minds, possible worlds.** Cambridge, MA: Harvard University Press.

Buchanan, M. (2013). **England's mental health services 'in crisis'.** [Online] http://www.bbc.co.uk/news/health-24537304 [Accessed: 03/02/2015].

Buckingham, David. (2008). **Introducing identity. Youth, identity, and digital media.** Edited by David Buckingham. The John D. and Catherine T. MacArthur Foundation Series on Digital Media and Learning. Cambridge, MA: MIT Press.

Budd, R., and Hughes, I. (2009). **The dodo bird verdict – Controversial, inevitable and important: A commentary on 30 years of meta-analyses.** Clinical Psychology & Psychotherapy. 16, 510–522. DOI: 10.1002/cpp.648.

Burgess, P., Pirkis, J., Coombs, T., and Rosen, A. (2011). **Assessing the value of existing recovery measures for routine use in Australian mental health services.** Australian and New Zealand Journal of Psychiatry, 45 (4), 267–280.

Burnard, P. (2007). **Seeing the psychiatrist: An autoethnographic account.** Journal of Psychiatric and Mental Health Nursing, 14, 808–813.

Burns, T., Catty, J., White, S., Becker, T., Koletsi, M., Fioritti, A., Rossler, W., Tomov, T., van Busschbach, J., Wiersma, D., and Lauber C. (2009). **The impact of supported employment and working on clinical and social functioning: Results of an international study of individual placement and support.** Schizophrenia Bulletin, 35 (5), 949–958.

Burns, T., and Molodynski, A. (2014). **Community treatment orders: Background and implications of OCTET trial.** Psychiatric Bulletin, 38, 3–5.

Burton, M., and Osorio, J.M.F. (2011). **Introducing Dussel: The philosophy of liberation and a really social psychology.** Psychology in Society, 41, 20–39.

Campbell, M.L.C., and Morrison, A.P. (2007). **The subjective experience of paranoia: Comparing the experiences of patients with psychosis and individuals with no psychiatric history.** Clinical Psychology and Psychotherapy, 14, 63–77.

Campbell, R., Pound, P., Pope, C., Britten, N., Pill, R., Morgan, M., and Donovan, J. (2003). **Evaluating meta-ethnography: A synthesis of qualitative research on lay experiences of diabetes and diabetes care.** Social Science and Medicine, 56 (4), 671–684.

Carless, D. (2008). **Narrative, identity, and recovery from serious mental illness: A life history of a runner.** Qualitative Research in Psychology, 5 (4), 233–248.

Carlisle, S., and Hanlon, P. (2008). **Well-being as a focus for public health? A critique and defence.** Critical Public Health, 18 (3), 263–270.

Cascardi, M., Mueser, K.T., DeGiralomo, J., and Murrin, M. (1996). **Physical aggression against inpatients by family members and partners.** Psychiatric Services, 47, 531–533.

Cavelti, M., Kvrgic, S., Beck, E.M., Kossowsky, J., and Vauth, R. (2012). **Assessing recovery from schizophrenia as an individual process: A review of self-report instruments.** European Psychiatry, 27, 19–32.

Chadwick, P., Hughes, S., Russell, D., Russell, I., and Dagnan, D. (2009). **Mindfulness groups for distressing voices and paranoia: A replication and randomized feasibility trial.** Behavioural and Cognitive Psychotherapy, 37 (4), 403–412.

Chadwick, P., Newman Taylor, K., and Abba, N. (2005). **Mindfulness groups for people with psychosis.** Behavioural and Cognitive Psychotherapy, 33 (3), 351–359.

Chin, J.T., Hayward, M., and Drinnan, A. (2009). **'Relating' to voices: Exploring the relevance of this concept to people who hear voices.** Psychology and Psychotherapy: Theory, Research and Practice, 82, 1–17.

Chisholm, B., Freeman, D., and Cooke, A. (2006). **Identifying potential predictors of traumatic reactions to psychotic episodes.** British Journal of Clinical Psychology, 45, 545–559.

Churchland, P.M. (1988). **'Folk psychology and the explanation of human behavior', A neurocomputational perspective.** Cambridge, MA: MIT Press.

Citizens Advice Bureau. (2010). **Not working: CAB evidence on ESA work capability assessment.** London: Author.

Clarke, Samantha P., Crowe, Trevor P., Oades, Lindsay G., and Deane, Frank P. (2009). **Do goal-setting interventions improve the quality of goals in mental health services?** Psychiatric Rehabilitation Journal, 32 (4), 292–299.

Clifton, A., Reynolds, J., Remnant, J., and Noble, J. (2013). **The age of austerity: The impact of welfare reform on people in the North East of England.** Mental Health Nursing, 33 (6), 30–32.

Coleman, R. (1999). **Recovery: An alien concept?** Gloucester: Handsell Publishing.

Corbin, J.M., and Strauss, A.L. (2008). **Basics of qualitative research: Techniques and procedures for developing grounded theory.** Los Angeles: Sage.

Corlett, P.R., Frith, C.D., and Fletcher, P.C. (2009). **From drugs to deprivation: A Bayesian framework for understanding models of psychosis.** Psychopharmacology, 206, 515–530.

Corrigan, P.W., Salzer, M., Ralph, R.O., Sangster, Y., and Keck, L. (2004). **Examining the factor structure of the recovery assessment scale.** Schizophrenia Bulletin, 30 (4), 1035–1041.

Coudert, F.R. (1939). **Proceedings of the Academy of Political Science, 1939.** New York: Columbia University Press.

Couley, A., and Oades, L.G. (2007). **SNAP Gippsland: A recovering team.** New Paradigm, June, 61–64.

Crossley, M.L. (2000). **Narrative psychology, trauma and the study of self/identity.** Theory and Psychology, 10 (4), 527–546.

Crowe, T.P., Deane, F.P., Oades, L.G., Caputi, P., and Morland, K.G. (2006). **Effectiveness of a collaborative recovery training program in Australia in promoting positive views about recovery.** Psychiatric Services, 57 (10), 1–5.

Daig, I., Herschbach, P., Lehmann, A., Knoll, N., and Decker, O. (2009). **Gender and age differences in domain-specific life satisfaction and the impact of depressive and anxiety symptoms: A general population survey from Germany**. Quality of Life Research, 18, 669–678.

Davidson, L., O'Connell, M., Tondora, J., Styron T., and Kangas, K. (2006). **The top ten concerns about recovery encountered in mental health system transformation**. Psychiatric Services, 57, 640–645.

Davidson, L., and Roe, D. (2007). **Recovery from versus recovery in serious mental illness: One strategy for lessening confusion plaguing recovery**. Journal of Mental Health, 16 (4), 459–470.

Davidson, L., and Strauss, J.S. (1992). **Sense of self in recovery from severe mental illness**. British Journal of Medical Psychology, 65 (2), 131–145.

Dawkins, R. (2011). **The magic of reality: How we know what's really true**. New York: Free Press.

Deikman, A.J. (1982). **The observing self**, Boston: Beacon Press.

Dennett, D. (1991). **Consciousness explained**. New York: Penguin.

Department of Health (DOH). (2001). **The journey to recovery – The government's vision for mental health care**. London: Author.

Department of Health (DOH). (2006). **From values to action: The chief nursing officer's review of mental health nursing**. London: Author.

Department of Health (DOH). (2009). **New horizons: A shared vision for mental health**. London: HM Government.

Department of Health (DOH). (2011). **No health without mental health: A cross-governmental mental health outcomes strategy for people of all ages**. London: HM Government.

DeSilva, D. (2011). **Helping people help themselves: A review of the evidence considering whether it is worthwhile to support self-management**. London: The Health Foundation.

Dilks, S., Tasker, F., and Wren, B. (2010). **Managing the impact of psychosis: A grounded theory exploration of recovery processes in psychosis**. British Journal of Clinical Psychology, 49 (1), 87–107.

Dill, D., Chu, J., Grob, M., and Eisen, S. (1991). **The reliability of abuse history reports**. Comprehensive Psychiatry, 32, 166–169.

Dunn, E.C., Rogers, E.S., Hutchinson, D.S., Lyass, A., MacDonald Wilson, K.L., Wallace, L.R., and Furlong-Norman, K. (2008). **Results of an innovative university-based recovery education program for adults with psychiatric disabilities**. Administrative Policy in Mental Health, 35 (5), 357–369.

Dupre, J. (1993). **The disorder of things. Metaphysical foundations of the disunity of science**. Cambridge, MA: Harvard University Press.

Dussel, E. (1995). **The invention of the Americas: Eclipse of 'the other' and the myth of modernity**. New York: Continuum.

Duval, S., and Tweedie, R. (2000). **Trim and fill: A simple funnel-plot-based method of testing and adjusting for publication bias in meta-analysis**. Biometrics, 56 (2), 455–463.

Eckersley, R., 2006. **Well and good: Morality, meaning and happiness**. Melbourne: Text Publishing.

Ehlers, A., and Clark, D.M. (2000). **A cognitive model of posttraumatic stress disorder**. Behaviour Research and Therapy, 38, 319–345.

Fisher, P., and Wells, A. (2005). **Experimental modification of beliefs in obsessive-compulsive disorder: A test of the metacognitive model**. Behaviour Research and Therapy, 43, 821–829.

Fisher, P., and Wells, A. (2008). **Psychological models of worry and generalized anxiety disorder**. In M. Antony and M. Stein (eds.), Handbook of Anxiety and the Anxiety Disorders. Oxford: Oxford University Press, 225–237.

Fletcher, P.C., and Frith, C.D. (2009). **Perceiving is believing: A Bayesian approach to explaining the positive symptoms of schizophrenia**. Nature, 10, 48–59.

Fodor, J. (1974). **Special sciences (Or: The disunity of science as a working hypothesis)**. Synthese, 28, 97–115.

Fodor, J. (1976). **The language of thought**. Cambridge, MA: Harvard University Press.

Foster, K., McAllister, M., and O'Brien, L. (2006). **Extending the boundaries: Autoethnography as an emergent method in mental health nursing research**. International Journal of Mental Health Nursing, 15, 44–53.

Foucault, M. (1980). **Power/knowledge: Selected interviews and other writings**. Edited by C. Gordon. Brighton: Harvester.

Fowler, D., Garety, P., and Kuipers, E. (1995). **Cognitive behavioural therapy for psychosis: Theory and practice**. Chichester: Wiley.

Fox, N.J. (2011). **The ill-health assemblage: Beyond the body-with-organs**. Health Sociology Review, 20 (4), 359–371.

Freeman, D., Freeman, J., and Garety, P. (2006). **Overcoming paranoid and suspicious thoughts**. London: Robinson Constable.

Freeman, D., and Garety, P.A. (2003). **Connecting neurosis and psychosis: The direct influence of emotion on delusions and hallucinations**. Behaviour Research and Therapy, 41, 923–947.

Freeman, D., and Garety, P.A. (2006). **Helping patients with paranoid and suspicious thoughts: The cognitive-behavioural approach**. Advances in Psychiatric Treatment, 12, 404–415.

Freeman, D., Garety, P., Kuipers, E., and Fowler, D. (2002). **A cognitive model of persecutory delusions**. British Journal of Clinical Psychology, 41, 331–347.

Frith, C.D. (1992). **The cognitive neuropsychology of schizophrenia**. Mahwah, NJ: Laurence Erlbaum.

Garety, P.A., and Freeman, D. (1999). **Cognitive approaches to delusions: A critical review of theories and evidence**. British Journal of Clinical Psychology, 38, 113–154.

Garety, P.A., Hemsley, D.R., and Wessely, S. (1991). **Reasoning in deluded schizophrenic and paranoid patients: Biases in performance on a probabilistic inference task.** Journal of Nervous and Mental Disease, 179, 194–201.

Gaudiano, B.A., and Herbert, J.D. (2006). **Acute treatment of inpatients with psychotic symptoms using Acceptance and Commitment Therapy: Pilot results.** Behavior Research Therapy, 44, 415–437.

Gee, L., Pearce, E., and Jackson, M. (2003). **Quality of life in schizophrenia: A grounded theory approach.** Health and Quality of Life Outcomes, 1, 1–11.

Gilbert, P. (2009). **The compassionate mind.** London: Constable and Robinson.

Glass, G.V., McGaw, B., and Smith, M.L. (1981). **Meta-analysis in social research.** Beverly Hills, CA: Sage.

Glatt, S.J., Faraone, S.V., and Tsuang, M.T. (2007). **Genetic risk factors for mental disorders: General principles and state of the science.** In M.T. Tsuang, W.S. Stone and M.J. Lyons (eds.), Recognition and Prevention of Major Mental and Substance Use Disorders. Washington, DC: American Psychiatric Publishing, 3–20.

Goodman, B., and Ley, T. (2012). **Psychology and sociology in nursing.** London: Sage.

Grant, A. (2009). **Evidence-based practice and the need for paradigmatic pluralism in cognitive behavioural psychotherapy.** Journal of Psychiatric and Mental Health Nursing, 16, 368–375.

Grant, A. (2011). **A critique of the representation of human suffering in the cognitive behavioural therapy literature with implications for mental health nursing practice.** Journal of Psychiatric Mental Health Nursing, 18 (1), 35–40.

Grant, A. (2013). **Troubling 'lived experience': A post-structural critique of mental health nursing qualitative research assumptions.** Journal of Psychiatric Mental Health Nursing, 21 (6), 544–549.

Grant, A.M., and Cavanagh, M.J. (2007). **Evidence-based coaching: Flourishing or languishing?** Australian Psychologist, 42 (4), 239–254.

Grant, A., and Leigh-Phippard, H. (2014). **Troubling the normative mental health recovery project: The silent resistance of a disappearing doctor.** In L. Zeeman, K. Aranda and A. Grant (eds.), Queering Health: Critical Challenges to Normative Health and Healthcare. Ross-on-Wye: PCCS Books, 100–115.

Grant, A., Short, N.P., and Turner, L. (2013). **Introduction: Storying life and lives.** In N.P. Short, L. Turner and A. Grant (eds.), Contemporary British Autoethnography. Rotterdam, Boston and Taipei: Sense Publishers, 1–16.

Grant, A., Townend, M., Mulhern R., and Short, N. (2010). **Cognitive behavioural therapy in mental health care** (2nd ed.). Beverly Hills, CA: Sage.

Grasemann, U., Hoffman, R.E., Gueorguieva, R., Quinlan, D., Lane, D., and Miikkulainen, R. (2010). **Evaluating computational models of language disturbance in schizophrenia.** BMC Neuroscience, 11 (1), 99.

Green, L.S., Oades, L.G., and Grant, A.M. (2006). **Cognitive-behavioural, solution focused life coaching: Enhancing goal striving, well-being and hope.** Journal of Positive Psychology, 1 (3), 142–149.

Gurney, K. (1997). **An introduction to neural networks.** London: University College London Press.

Haddock, G., and Lewis, S. (1996). **New psychological treatments in schizophrenia.** Advances in Psychiatric Treatment, 2, 110–116.

Hanisch, C. (1970). **The personal is political.** In S. Firestone and A. Koedt (eds.), Notes From the Second Year: Women's Liberation Major Writings of the Radical Feminists. New York: Radical Feminism.

Harding, C.M., Brooks, G.W., Ashikaga, T., Strauss, J.S., and Breier, A. (1987). **The Vermont Longitudinal Study of Persons with Severe Mental Illness, II: Long-term outcome of subjects who retrospectively met DSM-III criteria for schizophrenia.** American Journal of Psychiatry, 144, 727–735.

Harrow, M., and Jobe, T.H. (2013). **Does long-term treatment of schizophrenia with antipsychotic medications facilitate recovery?** Schizophrenia Bulletin, 39 (5), 962–965.

Hayes, S.C. (2004). **Acceptance and commitment therapy, relational frame theory, and the third wave of behavioural and cognitive therapies.** Behavior Therapy, 35, 639–665.

Health and Social Care Act 2012, c7. [Online] http://www.legislation.gov.uk/ukpga/2012/7/contents/enacted [Accessed: 03/02/2015].

Health and Social Care Information Centre. (2009). **Inpatients formally detained in hospitals under the Mental Health Act, 1983 and patients subject to supervised community treatment – 1998–1999 to 2008–2009.** [Online] http://www.hscic.gov.uk/article/2021/Website-Search?productid=13209&q=rates+of+CTO%27s+2007&sort=Relevance&size=10&page=1&area=both#top [Accessed: 30/06/2014].

Health and Social Care Information Centre. (2013). **Inpatients formally detained in hospitals under the Mental Health Act, 1983 and patients subject to supervised community treatment, England – 2012–2013.** [Online] http://www.hscic.gov.uk/article/2021/Website-Search?productid=13209&q=rates+of+CTO%27s+2007&sort=Relevance&size=10&page=1&area=both#top [Accessed: 30/06/2014].

Helliwell, J.F., and Putnam, R.D. (2004). **The social context of well-being.** Philosophical Transactions of the Royal Society B, 359, 1435–1446.

Henderson, C., Flood, C., Leese, M., Thornicroft, G., Sutherby, K., and Szmukler, G. (2004). **Effect of joint crisis plans on use of compulsory treatment in psychiatry: Single blind randomised controlled trial.** BMJ, 329, 136–138.

Herman, J., and Schatzow, E. (1987). **Recovery and verification of childhood sexual trauma.** Psychoanalytical Psychology, 4, 1–14.

Huppert, F.A. (2009). **Psychological well-being: Evidence regarding its causes and consequences.** Applied Psychology: Health and Well-Being, 1, 137–164.

Hutton, P., Morrison, A.P., Wardle, M., and Wells, A. (2014). **Metacognitive therapy in treatment-resistant psychosis. A multiple-baseline study.** Behavioural and Cognitive Psychotherapy, 42 (2), 166–185.

Iyengar, S., and Greenhouse, J.B. (1988). **Selection models and the file drawer problem.** Statistical Science, 3 (1), 109–117.

Jacobson, N.S., and Truax, P. (1991). **Clinical significance: A statistical approach to defining meaningful change in psychotherapy research.** Journal of Consulting and Clinical Psychology, 59 (1), 12–19.

Jaspers, K. (1962). **General psychopathology.** Translated by J. Hoenig and M.W. Hamilton. Manchester: Manchester University Press.

Jaynes, Julian. (1976). **The origin of consciousness in the breakdown of the bicameral mind.** Boston: Houghton Mifflin.

Job, D.E., Whalley, H.C., Johnstone, E.C., and Lawrie, S.M. (2005). **Grey matter changes over time in high risk subjects developing schizophrenia.** Neuroimage, 25 (4), 1023–1030.

Jones, C., Hacker, D., Cormac, I., Meaden, A., and Irving, C.B. (2012). **Cognitive behavioural therapy versus other psychosocial treatments for schizophrenia.** Cochrane Database of Systematic Reviews, 4, art. no. CD008712. DOI: 10.1002/14651858.CD008712.pub2.

Kabat-Zinn, J. (1994). **Wherever you go, there you are: Mindfulness meditation in everyday life.** New York: Hyperion.

Kapur, S. (2003). **Psychosis as a state of aberrant salience: A framework linking biology, phenomenology, and pharmacology in schizophrenia.** American Journal of Psychiatry, 160 (1), 13–23.

Keltner, D., and Haidt, J. (1999). **Social functions of emotions at four levels of analysis.** Cognition and Emotion, 13 (5), 505–521.

Kerr, C.E., Josyula K., and Littenberg R. (2012). **Developing an observing attitude: A qualitative analysis of meditation diaries in a MBSR clinical trial.** Clinical Psychology and Psychotherapy, 18 (1), 80–93.

Keyes, C.L.M. (1998). **Social well-being.** Social Psychology Quarterly, 61 (2), 121–140.

Keyes, C.L.M. (2002). **The mental health continuum: From languishing to flourishing in life.** Journal of Health and Social Behaviour, 43 (2), 207–222.

Keyes, C.L.M. (2005). **Mental illness and/or mental health? Investigating axioms of the complete state model of health.** Journal of Consulting and Clinical Psychology, 73 (3), 539–548.

Keyes, C.L.M. (2006). **Subjective wellbeing in mental health and human development research worldwide: An introduction.** Social Indicators Research, 77, 1–10.

Kingdon, D. (2010). **Over-simplification and exclusion of non-conforming studies can demonstrate absence of effect: A lynching party? A commentary on 'Cognitive behavioural therapy for major psychiatric disorder: Does it really work? A meta-analytical review of well-controlled trials' by Lynch et al.** Psychological Medicine, 40, 25–27.

Kingdon, D.G., and Kirschen, H. (2006). **Who does not get cognitive-behavioural therapy for schizophrenia when therapy is readily available?** Psychiatric Services, 57 (12), 1792–1794.

Kingdon, D.G., and Turkington, D. (2005). **Cognitive therapy of schizophrenia.** New York: Guilford Press.

Kings College London. (2013). **50th Maudsley Debate: CBT for psychosis.** [Online] http://www.kcl.ac.uk/ioppn/news/special-events/maudsley-debates/debate-archive-31-50.aspx [Accessed 08/05/2015].

Kisely, S., Preston, N., Xiao, J., Lawrence, D., Louise, S., Crowe, E., and Segal, S. (2013). **An eleven-year evaluation of the effect of community treatment orders on changes in mental health service use.** Journal of Psychiatric Research, 47, 650–656.

Laithwaite, H., and Gumley, A. (2007). **Sense of self, adaptation and recovery in patients with psychosis in a forensic NHS setting.** Clinical Psychology and Psychotherapy, 14, 302–316.

Lakeman, R. (2004). **Standardized routine outcome measurement: Pot holes in the road to recovery.** International Journal of Mental Health Nursing, 13, 210–225.

Langer, A.I., Cangas, A.J., Salcedo, E., and Fuentes, B. (2012). **Applying mindfulness therapy in a group of psychotic individuals: A controlled study,** Behavioural and Cognitive Psychotherapy, 40, 105–109.

Layard, R. (2005). **Happiness: Lessons from a new science.** New York and London: Penguin.

Leamy, M., Bird, V., Le Boutillier, C., Williams, J., and Slade, M. (2011). **Conceptual framework for personal recovery in mental health: Systematic review and narrative synthesis.** British Journal of Psychiatry, 199, 445–452.

Le Boutillier, C., Leamy, M., Bird, V.J., Davidson, L., Williams, J., and Slade, M. (2011). **What does recovery mean in practice? A qualitative analysis of international recovery-oriented practice guidance.** Psychiatric Services, 62 (12), 1470–1476.

Leucht, S., Arbter, D., Engel, R.R., Kissling, W., and Davis, J.M. (2009). **How effective are second-generation antipsychotic drugs? A meta-analysis of placebo-controlled trials.** Molecular Psychiatry, 14, 429–447.

Lieberman, J.E., Bymastrt, F.P., Meltzer, H.Y., Deutch, A.Y., Duncan, G.E., Marx, C.E., Aprille, J.R., Dwyer, D.S., Li, X., Mahadik, S.P., Duman, R.S., Porter, J.H., Modica-Napolitano, J.S., Newton, S.S., and Csernansky, J.G. (2008). **Antipsychotic drugs: Comparison in animal models of efficacy, neurotransmitter regulation and neuroprotection.** Pharmacological Reviews, 60 (3), 358–403.

Light, E. (2014). **The epistemic challenges of CTOs: Commentary on community treatment orders.** Psychiatric Bulletin, 38, 6–8.

Lillienfeld, S.O., and Arkowitz, H. (2011). **Can positive thinking be negative?** Scientific American. [Online] http://www.scientificamerican.com/article/can-positive-thinking-be-negative/ [Accessed: 01/07/2014].

Lindner, A., Their, P., Kircher, T.T., Haarmeier, T., and Leube, D.T. (2005). **Disorders of agency in schizophrenia correlate with an inability to compensate for the sensory consequences of actions.** Current Biology, 15, 1119–1124.

Linehan, M.M. (1987). **Dialectical behavioural therapy: A cognitive-behavioural approach to parasuicide.** Journal of Personality Disorders, 1, 328–333.

Link, B.G., Struening, E.L., Neese-Todd, S., Asmussen, S., and Phelan, J.C. (2001). **The consequences of stigma for the self-esteem of people with mental illness.** Psychiatric Services, 52, 1621–1626.

Locke, E.A., and Latham, G.P. (1990). **A theory of goal setting and task performance.** Englewood Cliffs, NJ: Prentice Hall.

Longden, E. (2013). **The voices in my head.** TED Talk [Online] http://www.ted.com/talks/eleanor_longden_the_voices_in_my_head [Accessed: 01/07/2014].

Lynch, D., Laws, K.R., and McKenna, P.J. (2010). **Cognitive Behavioural Therapy for major psychiatric disorder: Does it really work? A meta-analytical review of well-controlled studies.** Psychological Medicine, 40, 9–24.

Lysaker, P.H., Davis, L.D., Lightfoot, J., Hunter, N., and Strasburger, A. (2005). **Association of neurocognition, anxiety, positive and negative symptoms with coping preference in schizophrenia spectrum disorders.** Schizophrenia Research, 80, 163–171.

Lysaker, P.H., Roe, D., and Yanos, P.T. (2007). **Toward understanding the insight paradox: Internalized stigma moderates the association between insight and social functioning, hope and self-esteem among people with schizophrenia spectrum disorders.** Schizophrenia Bulletin, 33, 192–199.

Maher, B.A. (1974). **Delusional thinking and perceptual disorder.** Journal of Individual Psychology, 30, 98–113.

Maher, B.A. (1988). **Anomalous experience and delusional thinking: The logic of explanations.** In T.F. Oltmanns and B.A. Maher (eds.), Delusional Beliefs. Chichester: Wiley, 15–33.

Mancini, M. (2007). **The role of self-efficacy in recovery from serious psychiatric disabilities.** Qualitative Social Work, 6 (1), 49–74.

Mapplebeck, C. (2010). **Personal experiences of psychosis: Recovery and growth.** Presentation to Recovery Research Network, 21 October 2010. [Online] http://www.researchintorecovery.com/Mapplebeck%20Personal%20experiences%20of%20psychosisx%20[Read-Only].pdf [Accessed: 10/7/2012].

Marshall, S. (2008). **Mental health consumers' evaluation of recovery-oriented service provision.** PhD thesis, School of Psychology, University of Wollongong, Thesis Collection. [Online] http://ro.uow.edu.au/theses/824 [Accessed 08/05/2015].

Marshall, S., Oades, L.G., and Crowe, T.P. (2009). **Mental health consumers' perceptions of receiving recovery-focused services.** Journal of Evaluation in Clinical Practice, 15 (4), 654–659.

Martin, J.K., Pescosolido, B.A., and Tuch, S.A. (2000). **Of fear and loathing: The role of 'disturbing behavior', labels and causal attributions in shaping public attitudes toward people with mental illness.** Journal of Health and Social Behaviour, 41, 208–223.

McCabe, R., Leudar, I., and Antaki, C. (2004). **Do people with schizophrenia display theory of mind deficits in clinical interactions?** Psychological Medicine, 34, 401–412.

McCarthy-Jones, S., Marriott, M., Knowles, R.E., Rowse, G., and Thompson, A.R. (2013). **What is psychosis? A meta-synthesis of inductive qualitative studies exploring the experience of psychosis.** Psychosis: Psychological, Social and Integrative Approaches, 5, 1–16.

McGurk, S.R., Twamley, E.W., Sitzer, D.I., McHugo, G.J., and Mueser, K.T. (2007). **A meta-analysis of cognitive remediation in schizophrenia.** American Journal of Psychiatry, 164 (12), 1791–1802.

McKay, R.T., and Dennett, D.C. (2009). **The evolution of misbelief.** Behavioural and Brain Sciences, 32, 493–561.

Melo, S., Taylor, J., and Bentall, R.P. (2006). **'Poor me' versus 'bad me' paranoia and the instability of persecutory ideation.** Psychological Psychotherapy Theory, Research and Practice, 79, 271–287.

Mental Health Act. (1983/2007). London: Stationary Office. [Online] http://www.legislation.gov.uk/ukpga/2007/12/contents [Accessed: 30/06/2014].

Messari, S., and Hallam, R. (2003). **CBT for psychosis: A qualitative analysis of clients' experiences.** British Journal of Clinical Psychology, 42 (2), 171–188.

Minsky, M. (1981). **Music, mind, and meaning.** Computer Music Journal, 5 (3), 28–44.

Moncrieff, J. (2009). **A critique of the dopamine hypothesis of schizophrenia and psychosis.** Harvard Review of Psychiatry, 17, 214–225.

Morrison, A.P. (2001). **The interpretation of intrusions in psychosis: An integrative cognitive approach to hallucinations and delusions.** Behavioural and Cognitive Psychotherapy, 29, 257–276.

Morrison, A.P., Frame, L., and Larkin, W. (2003). **Relationships between trauma and psychosis: A review and integration.** British Journal of Clinical Psychology, 42, 331–353.

Morrison, A.P., Hutton, P., Shiers, D., and Turkington, D. (2012). **Antipsychotics: Is it time to introduce patient choice?** British Journal of Psychiatry, 201, 83–84.

Mueser, K.T., Corrigan, P.W., Hilton, D.W., Tanzman, B., Schaub, A., Gingerich, S., Essock, S.M., Tarrier, N., Morey, B., Vogel-Scibilia, S., and Herz, M.I. (2002). **Illness management and recovery: A review of the research.** Psychiatric Services, 53 (10), 1272–1284.

Mustafa, F. (2013). **On the OCTET and supervised community treatment orders.** Medicine, Science and the Law, 54 (2), 116–117. DOI:10.1177/0025802413506898.

National Institute of Health Care Excellence (NICE). (2009). **NICE Guidance CG82: Schizophrenia: Core interventions in the treatment and management of schizophrenia in adults in primary and secondary care.** London: Author.

Nursing and Midwifery Council. (2006). **Standards to support learning and assessment in practice: NMC standards for mentors, practice teachers and teachers**. London: Author.

Nursing and Midwifery Council. (2010). **Standards for pre-registration nursing education**. [Online] http://standards.nmc-uk.org/ [Accessed: 10/07/2015].

Oades, L.G., Crowe, T.P., and Nguyen, M. (2009). **Leadership coaching transforming mental health systems from the inside out: The Collaborative Recovery Model as person-centred strengths based coaching psychology**. International Coaching Psychology Review, 4 (1), 25–36.

O'Farrell, C. (2006). **Foucault and post modernism**. The Sydney Papers, 18 (3–4), 182–194.

Onken, S.J., Craig, C.M., Ridgway, P., Ralph, R.O., and Cook, J.A. (2007). **An analysis of the definitions and elements of recovery: A review of the literature**. Psychiatric Rehabilitation Journal, 31, 9–22.

Owen, M.J., Craddock, N., and Jablensky, A. (2007). **The genetic deconstruction of psychosis**. Schizophrenia Bulletin, 33 (4), 905–911.

Owen, M.J., O'Donovan, M.C., Thapar, A., and Craddock, N. (2011). **Neurodevelopmental hypothesis of schizophrenia**. British Journal of Psychiatry, 198 (3), 173–175.

Padesky, C.A. (1993). **Socratic questioning: Changing minds or guiding discovery?** Keynote address: European Congress of Behavioural and Cognitive Therapies, London, 24 September.

Padesky, C.A., Kuyken, W., and Dudley, R. (2011). **Collaborative case conceptualization: Working effectively with clients in Cogntive-Behavioural Therapy**. New York: Guilford Press.

Padesky, C.A., and Mooney, K.A. (2012). **Strengths-based cognitive behavioural therapy: A four-step model to build resilience**. Clinical Psychology and Psychotherapy, 19 (4), 283–290.

Peluso, M.J., Lewis, S.W., Barnes, T.R.E., and Jones, P.B. (2012). **Extrapyramidal motor side-effects of first- and second-generation antipsychotic drugs**. British Journal of Psychiatry, 200, 387–392.

Penades, R., and Catalan, R. (2012). **Cognitive remediation therapy (CRT): Improving neurocognition and functioning in schizophrenia**. In T.H.J. Byrne (ed.), Schizophrenia in the 21st Century. Rijeka, Croatia: InTech, 69–86.

Perkins, R., and Slade, M. (2012). **Recovery in England: Transforming statutory services?**, International Review of Psychiatry, 24 (1), 29–39.

Perner, J., (1991). **Understanding the representational mind**. Cambridge, MA: MIT Press.

Phillips, L.J., Francey, S.M., Edwards, J., and McMurray, N. (2009). **Strategies used by psychotic individuals to cope with life stress and symptoms of illness: A systematic review**. Anxiety, Stress and Coping, 22 (4), 371–410.

Piaget, J. (1964). **Part I: Cognitive development in children: Piaget development and learning**. Journal of Research in Science Teaching, 2 (3), 176–186.

Pinfold, V., Byrne, P., and Toulmin, H. (2005). **Challenging stigma and dis-crimination in communities: A focus group study identifying UK mental health service users' main campaign priorities**. International Journal of Social Psychiatry, 51 (2), 128–138.

Quine, W. (1969). **Natural kinds**. In W. Quine (ed.), Ontological Relativity and Other Essays. New York: Columbia University Press, 114–138.

Ratner, C. (2000). **Agency and culture**. Journal for The Theory of Social Behaviour, 30, 413–434.

Read, J., van Os, J., Morrison, A., and Ross, C.A. (2005). **Childhood trauma, psychosis and schizophrenia. A literature review with theoretical and clinical implications**. Acta Psychiatrica Scandinavica, 112, 330–350.

Redmond, C., Larkin, M., and Harrop, C. (2010). **The personal meaning of romantic relationships for young people with psychosis**. Clinical Child Psychology and Psychiatry, 15, 151–170.

Repper, J., and Carter, T. (2011). **A review of the literature on peer support in mental health services**. Journal of Mental Health, 20 (4), 392–411.

Repper, J., and Perkins, R. (2003). **Social inclusion and recovery**. London: Balliere Tindall.

Resnick, S.G., and Rosenheck, R.A. (2006). **Recovery and positive psychology: Parallel themes and potential synergies**. Psychiatric Services, 57, 120–122.

Resnick, S.G., Rosenheck, R.A., and Lehman, A.F. (2004). **An exploratory analysis of correlates of recovery**. Psychiatric Services, 55, 540–547.

Roberts, G., and Wolfson, P. (2004). **The rediscovery of recovery: Open to all**. Advances in Psychiatric Treatment, 10, 37–48.

Rocha, N.B.F, and Queiros, C. (2013). **Metacognitive and social cognition training (MSCT) in schizophrenia: A preliminary efficacy study**. Schizophrenia Research, 150 (1), 64–68.

Roe, D. (2001). **Progressing from patienthood to personhood across the multidimensional outcomes in schizophrenia and related disorders**. Journal of Nervous and Mental Disease, 189, 691–699.

Roets, G., Roose, R., Claes, L., Vandekinderen, C., Van Hove, G., and Vanderplasschen, W. (2012). **Reinventing the employable citizen: A perspective for social work**. British Journal of Social Work, 42, 94–110.

Rogers, C. (1980). **A way of being**. Boston: Houghton Mifflin.

Romme, M., and Escher, S. (1993). **Accepting voices.** London: Mind Publications.

Rose, D., Evans, J., Sweeney, A., and Wykes, T. (2011). **A model for developing outcome measures from the perspectives of mental health service users**. International Review of Psychiatry, 23 (1), 41–46.

Rosenthal, R. (1979). **The 'file drawer problem' and tolerance for null results**. Psychological Bulletin, 86 (3), 638–641.

Royal College of Psychiatrists, Care Services Improvement Partnership and Social Care Institute for Excellence. (2007). **A common purpose – Recovery in future mental health services**. Royal College of Psychiatrists. [Online] http://www.recoveryin-sight.com/a-common-purpose-recovery-in-future-mental-health-services/ [Accessed: 10/07/2015].

Royal College of Psychiatrists. (2012). **Mental health and growing up factsheet: Psychosis: Information for young people** [Online] http://www.rcpsych.ac.uk/pdf/Worries%20and%20anxieties%20for%20parents.pdf [Accessed: 10/7/2012].

Royal College of Psychiatrists. (2014). **Statement on mental health payment systems (formerly payment by results).** RCPysch. [Online] http://www.rcpsych.ac.uk/pdf/PS01_2014x.pdf [Accessed: 08/06/2015].

Ruggeri, M., Leese, M., Thornicroft, G., Bisoffi, G., and Tansella, M. (2000). **Definition and prevalence of severe and persistent mental illness.** British Journal of Psychiatry, 177, 149–155.

Rycroft-Malone, J. (2006). **Editorial.** Worldviews on Evidence-Based Nursing, 3, 1.

Salkovskis, P.M. (2002). **Empirically grounded clinical interventions: Cognitive-behavioural therapy progresses through a multi-dimensional approach to clinical science.** Behavioural and Cognitive Psychotherapy, 30, 3–9.

Salkovskis, P.M., Candida Richards, H., and Forrester, E. (1995). **The relationship between obsessional problems and intrusive thoughts.** Behavioural and Cognitive Psychotherapy, 23 (3), 281–299.

Sanders, A.R., Duan, J., Levinson, D.F., Shi, J., He, D., Hou, C., Burrell, G.J., Rice, J.P., Nertney, D.A., Olincy, A., Rozic, P., Vinogradov, S., Buccola, N.G., Mowry, B.J., Freedman, R., Amin, F., Black, D.W., Silverman, J.M., Byerley, W.F., Crowe, R.R., Cloninger, C.R., Martinez, M., and Gejman, P.V. (2008). **No significant association of 14 candidate genes with schizophrenia in a large European ancestry sample: Implications for psychiatric genetics.** American Journal of Pscyhiatry, 165 (4), 497–506. PMID 18198266.

Schiller, D., Monfils, Marie-H., Raio, Candace M., Johnson, David C., LeDoux, Joseph E., and Phelps, Elizabeth A. (2010). **Preventing the return of fear in humans using reconsolidation update mechanisms.** Nature, 463 (7277), 49–53.

Scourfield, P. (2009). **A critical reflection on the involvement of 'experts by experience' in inspections.** British Journal of Social Work, 40 (6), 1890–1907.

Seeman, P. (2002). **Atypical antipsychotics: Mechanism of action.** Canadian Journal of Psychiatry, 47 (1), 27–38.

Seligman, M.E.P., and Csikszentmihalyi, M. (2000). **Positive psychology: An introduction.** American Psychologist, 55 (1), 5–14.

Shapiro, S.L., Carlson, L.E., Astin, J.A., and Freedman, B. (2006). **Mechanisms of mindfulness.** Journal of Clinical Psychology, 3, 373–386.

Shepherd, G., Boardman, J., Rinaldi, M., and Roberts, G. (2014). **Supporting recovery in mental health services: Quality and outcomes.** London: Sainsbury Centre for Mental Health.

Shepherd, G., Boardman, J., and Slade, M. (2008). **Making recovery a reality.** London: Sainsbury Centre for Mental Health.

Sivec, H.J., and Montesano, V.L. (2012). **Cognitive behavioural therapy for psychosis in clinical practice.** Psychotherapy, 49 (2), 258–270.

Slade, M. (2009). **Personal recovery and mental illness: A guide for mental health professionals.** Cambridge: Cambridge University Press.

Slade, M. (2010). **Mental illness and well-being: The central importance of positive psychology and recovery approaches.** BMC Health Services Research, 10, 26.

Slade, M. (2012). **Recovery research: The empirical evidence from England.** World Psychiatry, 11, 162–163.

Slade, M., Amering, M., Farkas, M., Hamilton, B., O'Hagan, M., Panther, G., Perkins, R., Shepherd, G., Tse, S., and Whitley, R. (2014). **Uses and abuses of recovery: Implementing recovery-oriented practices in mental health systems.** World Psychiatry, 13 (1), 12–20.

Slade, M., Amering, M., and Oades, L.G. (2008). **Recovery: An international perspective.** Epidemiologia e Psichiatria Sociale, 17 (2), 128–137.

Slade, M., Bird, V., Le Boutillier, C., Williams, J., McCrone, P., and Leamy, M. (2011). **REFOCUS Trial: Protocol for a cluster randomised controlled trial of a pro-recovery intervention within community based mental health teams.** BMC Psychiatry, 11, 185.

Smieskova, R., Fusar-Poli, P., Allen, P., Bendfeldt, K., Stieglitz, R.D., Drewe, J., Radue, E.W., McGuire, P.K., Riecher-Rossler, A., and Borgwardt, S.J. (2009). **The effects of antipsychotics on the brain: What have we learnt from structural imaging of schizophrenia? – A systematic review.** Current Pharmaceutical Design, 15 (22), 2535–2549.

Sokal, A.D. (1996). **A physicist experiments with cultural studies.** Lingua Franca. [Online] http://www.physics.nyu.edu/faculty/sokal/lingua_franca_v4/lingua_franca_v4.html [Accessed: 07/01/2014].

Stevenson, A. (ed.). (2010). **Oxford Dictionary of English** (3rd ed.). Oxford: Oxford University Press.

Stirman, S.W., DeRubeis, R.J., Crits-Christoph, P., and Rothman, A. (2005). **Can the randomized controlled trial literature generalize to nonrandomized patients?** Journal of Consulting and Clinical Psychology, 73, 127–135.

Strous, R.D., Ratner, Y., Gibel, A., Ponizovsky, A., and Ritsner, M. (2005). **Longitudinal assessment of coping abilities at exacerbation and stabilization in schizophrenia.** Comprehensive Psychiatry, 46, 167–175.

Tait, L., and Lester, H. (2005). **Encouraging user involvement in mental health services.** Advances in Psychiatric Treatment, 11, 168–175.

Tandon, R., Keshavan, M.S., and Nasrallah, H.A. (2008). **Schizophrenia, "just the facts": What we know in 2008, Part 1: Overview.** Schizophrenia Research, 100, 4–19.

Taylor, C. (1989). **Sources of the self.** Cambridge: Cambridge University Press.

Taylor, S., Leigh-Phippard, H., and Grant, A. (2014). **Writing for recovery: A practice development project for mental health service users, carers and survivors.** International Practice Development Journal, 4 (1), 1–13.

Tellegen, A., Watson, D., and Clark, L.A. (1999). **On the dimensional and hierarchical structure of affect.** Psychological Science, 10 (4), 297–303.

Tew, J., Ramon, S., Slade, M., Bird, V., Melton, J., and LeBoutillier, C. (2012). **Social factors and recovery from mental health difficulties: A review of the evidence.** British Journal of Social Work, 42 (3), 443–460.

Viguera, A.C., Baldessarini, R.J., Hegarty, J.D., van Kammen, D.P., and Tohen, M. (1997). **Clinical risk following abrupt and gradual withdrawal of maintenance neuroleptic treatment.** Archives of General Psychiatry, 54, 49–55.

Vygotsky, L.S. (1998). **The collected works of L.S. Vygotsky,** Vol. 5. Edited by Robert W. Rieber and Marie J. Hall. New York: Plenum Press.

Wagner, L.C., and King, M. (2005). **Existential needs of people with psychotic disorders in Parto Alegre, Brazil.** British Journal of Psychiatry, 186, 141–145.

Warner, R. (2009). **Recovery from schizophrenia and the recovery model.** Current Opinion in Psychiatry, 22, 374–380.

Watson, A.C., Corrigan, P., Larson, J.E., and Sells, M. (2007). **Self-stigma in people with mental illness.** Schizophrenia Bulletin, 33, 1312–1318.

Watson, D.P. (2012). **The evolving understanding of recovery: What the sociology of mental health has to offer.** Humanity and Society, 36 (4), 290–308.

Weatherhead, S., Delaney, M., Weston, J., Williams, S., Mozo-Dutton, L., Chapman, C., Chen, C., Clarke, A., Gray, S., Svanberg, J., Stuart, S., Bazen-Peters, C., Blackwell, H., Judge, J., Fugard, A., Jenkins, K.G., Berry, A., Adair-Stantiall, A., Bancroft, V., Reynolds, F., Rahim, M., Coetzer, R., Black, J., Eccles, F., and Boothroyd, G. (2014). **Written evidence submitted to commons select committee: Employment and support allowance and work capability assessments inquiry.** [Online] http://www.parliament.uk/business/committees/committees-a-z/commons-select/work-and-pensions-committee/inquiries/parliament-2010/esa-wca-inq-2014/?type=Written#pnlPublication Filter [Accessed: 09/04/2014].

Wells, A. (2009). **Metacognitive therapy for anxiety and depression.** New York: Guilford Press.

Wells, A., and Papageorgiou, C. (1998). **Relationships between worry, obsessive-compulsive symptoms and meta-cognitive beliefs.** Behaviour Research and Therapy, 36 (9), 899–913.

White, M. (1995). **Re-authoring lives: Interviews and essays.** Dulwich Centre Publications.

Williams, J., Leamy, M., Bird, V., Harding, C., Larsen, J., Le Boutillier, C., Oades, L., and Slade, M. (2012). **Measures of the recovery orientation of mental health services: Systematic review.** Social Psychiatry and Psychiatric Epidemiology, 47, 1827–1835.

Woods, S.W., Addington, J., Cadenhead, K.S., Cannon, T.D., Cornblatt, B.A., Heinssen, R., Perkins, D.O., Seidman, L.J., Tsuang, M.T., Walker, E.F., and McGlashan, T.H. (2009). **Validity of the prodromal risk syndrome for first** psychosis: Findings from the North American Prodrome Longitudinal Study. Schizophrenia Bulletin, 35 (5), 894–908.

World Health Organisation (WHO). (1946). **Official records of the World Health Organisation no 2: Proceedings and final acts of the International Health Conference**. United Nations WHO Interim Commission.

World Health Organisation (WHO). (1992). **International statistical classification of diseases and related health problems** (10th revision). Geneva: Author.

Wright, E.R., Gronfein, W.P., and Owens, T.J. (2000). **Deinstitutionalization, social rejection, and the self-esteem of former mental patients**. Journal of Health and Social Behavior, 41, 68–90.

Wunderink, L., Nieboer, R.M., Wiersma, D., Sytema, S., and Nienhuis, F.J. (2013). **Recovery in remitted first-episode psychosis at 7 years of follow-up of an early dose reduction/discontinuation or maintenance treatment strategy: Long-term follow-up of a 2-year randomized clinical trial**. JAMA Psychiatry, 70 (9), 913–920. DOI: 10.1001/jamapsychiatry.2013.19.hard.

Wykes, T., Huddy, V., Cellard, C., McGurk, S.R., and Czobor, P. (2011). **A meta-analysis of cognitive remediation for schizophrenia: Methodology and effect sizes**. American Journal of Psychiatry, 168 (5), 472–485.

Yanos, P.T., Roe, D., and Lysaker, P.H. (2010). **The impact of illness identity on recovery from severe mental illness**. American Journal of Psychiatric Rehabilitation. 13 (2), 73–93.

Yorston, G. (2001). **Mania precipitated by meditation: A case report and literature review**. Mental Health, Religion and Culture, 4, 209–213.

Zimmerman, G., Favrod, J., Trieu, V.H., and Pomini, V. (2005). **The effect of cognitive behavioural treatment on the positive symptoms of schizophrenia spectrum disorders: A meta-analysis**. Schizophrenia Research, 77 (1), 1–9.

Zubin, J., and Spring, B. (1977). **Vulnerability – A new view of schizophrenia**. Journal of Abnormal Psychology, 86 (2),103–126.

Index